LAKE DISTRICT WALKS FOR MOTORISTS

Central Area

Warne Gerrard Guides for Walkers

Walks for Motorists Series

CHESHIRE WALKS

CHILTERNS WALKS
        Northern
        Southern

COTSWOLDS WALKS
        Northern
        Southern

EXMOOR WALKS

JERSEY WALKS

LAKE DISTRICT WALKS
        Central
        Northern
        Western

LONDON COUNTRYSIDE WALKS
        North West
        North East
        South West
        South East

GREEN LONDON WALKS
        (both circular and cross country)

MIDLAND WALKS

NORTH YORK MOORS WALKS
        North and East
        West and South

PEAK DISTRICT WALKS

PENDLESIDE AND BRONTE COUNTRY WALKS

SNOWDONIA WALKS
        Northern

SOUTH DOWNS WALKS

WYE VALLEY WALKS

YORKSHIRE DALES WALKS

FURTHER DALES WALKS

Long Distance and Cross Country Walks

WALKING THE PENNINE WAY

RAMBLES IN THE DALES

Warne Gerrard Guides for Walkers

LAKE DISTRICT

WALKS FOR MOTORISTS

CENTRAL AREA

John Parker

30 sketch maps by Tom Brodrick

FREDERICK WARNE

Published by
Frederick Warne (Publishers) Ltd.
40 Bedford Square,
London WC1B 3HE

© Frederick Warne (Publishers) Ltd. 1971

First published 1971
Reprinted 1972
Reprinted 1973
Reprinted (twice) 1974
Reprinted (twice) 1975
Reprinted (twice) 1976
Reprinted 1977
Reprinted 1978
Revised edition 1978
Second Revised edition 1979

The front cover picture is of Grasmere and Rydal and was taken by Tom Parker. The back cover picture of Rydal church is reproduced by permission of the British Tourist Authority, as are the inside pictures of Tarn Hows and Rydal Mount. The pictures of Hawkshead and Bridge House, Ambleside, were taken by Geoffrey Berry.

Publishers' Note

While every care has been taken in the compilation of this book, the publishers cannot accept responsibility for any inaccuracies. But things may have changed since the book was published: paths are sometimes diverted, a concrete bridge may replace a wooden one, stiles disappear. Please let the publishers know if you discover anything like this on your way.

The length of each walk in this book is given in miles and kilometres, but within the text Imperial measurements are quoted. It is useful to bear the following approximations in mind: 5 miles = 8 kilometres, ½ mile = 805 metres, 1 metre = 39.4 inches.

ISBN 0 7232 2155 3

Printed by Galava Printing Co. Ltd., Nelson, Lancashire

Contents

Introduction

This walkers' guide is not for athletes. It is for people who like to walk, or want to walk, in a leisurely way, enjoying to the full the natural beauty of Britain's largest National Park. It is for photographers, amateur naturalists, ornithologists, artists or just lingerers. The walks described can be enjoyed by young or old, or family parties.

Most guides are concerned with travelling from A to B. The decline of rural transport, and the increase in personal transport, now makes this sort of information impractical and unnecessary. The walks described here are from A to A: "A" being the reader's car.

This guide is not for fell walkers. Fine fell guides are already available. It is assumed that not all walkers are keen to accept the challenge of the high places. The author, himself a regular fell walker and an active member of mountain rescue, is only too well aware that an alarmingly high proportion of fell accidents happen to holidaymakers who are not equipped for, or prepared to face, fell expeditions. From the valleys the fell footpaths are clear for all to see. They can be a dangerous attraction. On the other hand, the valley and lake-shore footpaths are not so apparent. They start at farm gates, hide up private-looking drives and behind inns and churchyards. This guide explains where some good paths can be found and enjoyed.

Those who do not scramble up to the high fells miss out on little. Indeed, most fell walkers do not know what they are missing in the valleys. Some of the Lake District's finest views are from the lower levels and there is a greater wealth of scenic variety, and of natural history, to be seen in the lush sheltered dales. There are hundreds of miles of fine footpaths, some of them hardly discovered by modern generations and few of them mentioned in the current general guides to the district. Some of them can offer eye-feasts, and quiet pleasures beyond all telling.

RIGHTS OF WAY

All the walks described here are on official rights of way, or permissive footpaths, or on public access areas. Some guides have caused trouble and distress to landowners and farmers as they have encouraged trespass, and indirectly been the cause of damage to walls and fences. This guide describes officially designated paths and bridle-ways, the right of passage over which cannot properly be challenged. There is the proviso, however, that routes are legally changed from time to time by developments or road improvements; in which case the altered alignment should be signposted.

The rights are plain. The responsibilities should be recognised too. Right of passage across a farm field, for instance, does not mean a right to wander off the path to picnic. Grass is an important growing crop and is damaged by trampling. Dogs, to, need to be kept under proper control; and it is strongly recommended that every dog should be on a lead when passing through farmland. Even 'harmless' dogs, if they are boisterous and playful among farm stock, can cause harm. Farmers have a right to put an unlocked gate across a right of way. Walkers have a responsibility, after opening such a gate, to close it after them to prevent stock wandering. Litter—even sweet wrappings—should be taken back to the car.

Where there is free public access, and one can wander off the path at will, the guide usually mentions this.

EQUIPMENT

A map is not strictly necessary if this guide is carried, as the routes are described in detail and sketch-maps provided. All one needs to know is which is one's right hand and one's left. A one inch to the mile tourist map, or the metric 1:50,000 or the Ordnance Survey Outdoor Leisure map 1:25,000, however, adds interest, and helps identify points in distant prospects that are not mentioned. Such maps also are the best to show the local roads. A pocket compass is not necessary either but can also add interest.

The most important item is footwear but the comparatively expensive boots needed for the fells are not required here. Footwear should be well-fitting and reasonably waterproof. Ideally, to prevent blistering feet, boots should be worn over woollen socks. Completely smooth soles can be a misery as they slide on wet stones and dry grass, and they waste energy. Clothing should be comfortable and lightweight waterproofs should be carried.

Even if the intention is to be back at the car for a meal, some food should be pocketed in case you are delayed. The other, optional, equipment includes cameras, sketch pads, plant or bird indentification books and binoculars.

THE LAKE DISTRICT NATIONAL PARK AND THE NATIONAL TRUST

The whole of the Lake District from the A6 in the east to the coast of Cumbria in the west is a National Park—866 square miles. This does not mean that the whole of this land belongs to the nation and you can wander on it at will. It means that it is a very specially protected area where any unsightly development is prevented. Its governing body—the National Park Planning Board—

also has a duty to help the public to enjoy the amenities. The Board can, for instance, acquire land for public access and for car parks. It provides an information service, and the information centres can be found in some of the busier areas, Brockhole, the National Park Visitor Centre, is a house set among lovely gardens by the lake shore between Windermere and Ambleside. There is a permanent exhibition, and there are lectures and film shows illustrating all that the Lake District has to offer. It is well worth a visit.

In addition, the National Park has a Warden Service, with several professional wardens and a lot of weekend volunteers. They might be met on the footpaths and access areas described here, and can be recognised by their armbands, badges and car screen stickers. They are there to encourage good behaviour, to enforce by-laws and the litter act; but their main function is to be friendly and helpful. They are 'mobile information centres'.

The National Trust on the other hand, in spite of what its title might suggest, has nothing to do with government. It is a private body entirely supported by voluntary contributions. It exists to acquire land and property of historic importance, and of natural beauty, for its protection, and for the public to enjoy. By good fortune the National Trust is the largest landowner in the Lake District National Park. The National Park Planning Board and the National Trust operate together for the public good.

THE COUNTRY CODE

Your walks can be marred if you cause trouble to farmers, land-owners and fellow walkers but unpleasant encounters can be avoided given a little common-sense and imagination. Some of these points have been mentioned but are so important that they are repeated.

Litter is offensive and should never be left.

Dogs, even normally harmless friendly dogs, should be properly controlled, and leashed where necessary.

When encountering closed gates, they should be closed after you.

The other points of the country code are a matter of common sense, too. Keep to the paths. Avoid damaging dry-stone walls. Beware of contaminating drinking water. Respect other people's property, privacy and right to enjoy peace and quiet. Guard against risk of fire — especially in woodland. Resist the temptation to uproot or damage plants, ferns, shrubs or trees.

Last, but not least, drive carefully, and walk carefully, on the narrow country roads.

OBSTRUCTED RIGHTS OF WAY

If a right of way is obstructed if would be of service if the matter were reported with precise details and location to the National Park Officer, Lake District Planning Board, County Hall, Kendal.

Jenkyn Crag is one of the best viewpoints for the head of Windermere Lake. It can be reached by anyone, and a visit to it can be combined with an interesting round walk through Skelghyll woods.

Park your car at Waterhead Car Park, or the neighbouring public car park by the Regent Hotel. Both are at the head of the lake about ¾ mile south of Ambleside. Leave the car park towards the lake and walk left towards the pier; however, before reaching it turn left alongside the end of the Waterhead Hotel. If you stand here and look across the main Ambleside to Windermere road, you will see a gap in the wall, with steps, between the Romney Hotel on the right and the Ghyll Head Hotel left. This is the route. Cross the road with great care.

The path climbs between fences, on loose stones, and turns right when it reaches a wall. Soon the path ends at a step stile over the wall on the left. Go through this and cross the field. This is a farm field and not a public access area; there is a right of way across it only. The wall just ahead bends left, then right, and there is a stile near the corner similar to the last. Through this stile and you are in a National Trust woodland and you can wander at will; but our path is the one that bears right from the stile. It crosses a slate bridge and climbs through the wood — a hardwood mixture largely, of ash, oak, silver birch and alder. There are also a number of geans, or wild cherries in this wood; tree spotters should look for them. In Spring, white flowers and pink buds identify them; in Autumn their leaves vary from yellow, through orange, to red. The leaves are long with serrated edges, their bark similar to the silver birches, but reddish.

Continue up to a T junction by an iron seat. (A few yards before this path appears to cross the one you are on; ignore it.) Turn right along a very distinct track. There are now some conifers in the wood. The nearest at this point are Douglas Firs. The track turns left by a ghyll and ascends by rough crag steps.

A bridge is soon approached. Cross, and ignore the track left. There are now two tracks. The right-hand one is better after wet weather. The left-hand one has a gentler climb but is inclined to muddiness. The track presently falls, and then levels; then look for a wall gap to the right, with a path leading from it to a crag. There should be a National Trust sign at this point. Walk through and up to the crag through the trees, and you are on Jenkyn Crag. Take care how you walk if the rock is wet.

There is a good view of Windermere head from here, as far down

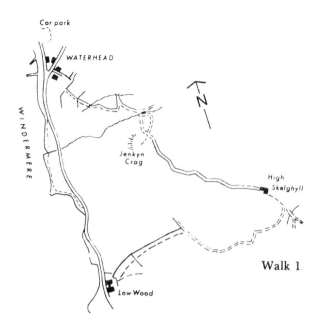

Walk 1

the lake as Belle Isle and Bowness. The tarn on the hillside opposite is Blelham Tarn, to the left of it is the cairned fell of Latterbarrow, and left again the woods of Claife Heights. The Coniston Old Man range is ahead in the background. To the right of this range is Wrynose Pass then Crinkle Crags, Pike o'Blisco, Bowfell, and to the right of that the Langdale Pikes. In front of this, and commanding the head of the lake, is Loughrigg Fell. To the left of Blelham Tarn, and below it, is Wray Castle, a fine example of the Victorian romantic era. The bogus ruins were demolished recently as they had become dangerous, but the main building still stands.

When you have lingered and enjoyed this view, leave the crag by the way you came, but on reaching the track turn right and ascend slightly. Presently the wood finishes on the right, and there is a view of the lake across open fields. The large hardwood which you should now see is a typical cherry — in case by now you have failed to find one. A little farther on you may well wonder at the two iron wicket gates, well maintained and locked, to right and left. Another such gate will be noticed down the field, right, and another in the wall next to it. This marks the way of the Manchester Corporation pipeline from Thirlmere reservoir. Someone at Manchester Town Hall had decreed that the gates should be regularly painted. They still are, even though the one on your left stands isolated, between two good gate-posts, from any wall or fence. There are a number of such lonely gates and one can wonder at the strange ways of local government; and probably ponder these questions: (a) does the area water authority inspector, walking the line, unlock *every* gate and re-lock, or does he craftily by-pass the lone ones? (b) Does he have a separate key for every lock? As we boggle at these vital problems, ascend to the gate across the track as the wood ends.

Beyond the gate there are again good views across to the lake. Go through two gates, through the farm-yard High Skelghyll and down the track. Go through another gate, and instead of turning left to cross the bridge over the ghyll, bear right along the track. Go through another gate and the track bends right away from the ghyll, towards the lake. This is a very pleasant walk through the fields but keep to the path as you are no longer on a public access area. The track bends left with a wall. A little farther on the track again bends left with the wall, but at this point we leave the track to descend to a less clearly-seen footpath towards the Low Wood Hotel which can be seen below. Just before the bend of the wall go through the gate on the right. The path follows a wall on the left, which presently has a crook in it, and there is a gate. Go through gate and go down towards the roofs of the hotel on an indistinct path. The path goes towards a wall, bends right to follow it, and then reaches the wall at a wooden ladder stile. Cross it. The path follows the wall down again, and as you descend a gate will be noticed in the wall ahead, to the left. Cross the corner of the field to it.

Through the gate follow the wall down, turn right through the gate in it, then left through gate into the Low Wood Hotel car park. Cross between the Low Wood buildings. The Low Wood Hotel was a popular stopping place for tourists in coaching days. Cross the road to the far sidewalk with very great care. Turn right. The walk now, along the side of the lake, would be pleasant but for the noise of the traffic on the road. You can get a little further from it by crossing the wall on the left just before the iron gate and walking along the lake shore. The way is soon criss-crossed by roots, and depending upon the height of the water, sooner or later you will be forced back onto the footpath by the road-side. Following this, the wood on the left ends and there is a green field down to the lake shore. This is in the care of the National Trust so you can make a pleasant detour here along the side of the water. There is a stile in the corner directly you come to the field. Go over it and along the lake shore. This is farmed, and dogs should be on leash. The crag on this shore marks the speed limit on the lake, for safety in the boat congestion at the waterhead. From the crag there is a good view across the Langdales. After the boathouse, ford or jump the stream and continue along the path towards the garage. If the stream is uncrossable, follow it up to the wall. The path turns up by the grange and through a stile onto the roadside footpath again. Follow the footpath on, and round left to Waterhead.

Walk to Brockhole, the National Park Centre, when you can drive right in? Well, why not? Before enjoying the permanent and varied exhibition there, or lounging about the gardens, why not walk along airy paths with long-distance views across the lake.

The route lies mainly over very old tracks, and one would imagine that they are just what the roads would have been like in the nineteenth century. Indeed, although Ambleside and Windermere are only a mile or two away, one could have the impression of stepping back into history. The main part of the walk is done before reaching Brockhole. The return walk is barely a mile, but as it is mainly uphill, plenty of time should be left to make it. Allow, say, forty-five minutes for the return. Actually the walk starts half a mile short of Townend, Troutbeck. Townend is a 17th century house in the care of the National Trust and open to the public.

To reach the starting point from Ambleside, take the Windermere road. Just after the Low Wood Hotel take the road off, up a steep hill, to the left, signposted 'Troutbeck'. Drive one mile, right to the top of the hill, taking the bends of this narrow road with care. When the road at last begins to fall there is a lane, unsurfaced, on the right, and just a little further on a green lay-by on the right. Pull in here without obstructing the gate. From Windermere, take the Ambleside road, and after the Sun Hotel in about a mile and a half, prepare to turn right. The turn is just over the bridge, on a bend, signposted 'Troutbeck'. Ascend this road, and in a mile and a half you reach the first turning left, a sharp one signposted 'Low Wood & Ambleside'. Turn up here. When the road levels out look for the green lay-by on the left. Park without obstructing the gate.

Leave the lay-by and walk up the lane which is almost opposite. This is a stony lane between walls. There are good views over Windermere, left, as you climb. The lane eventually reaches another track at a T junction. There is a seat here from which there is a good long view over Windermere. Sit down and enjoy it. After the climb you may need a rest. The lake appears to be cut in two by Belle Isle. Getting off the seat and facing the same way as when you arrived, turn left. The view, before long, is obscured after a track comes in from the left, as there is rising ground to the left, but the way remains pleasant. Now shortly after this you leave this track. This is at the point where the walls on either side open out, and the views of the lake appear again. Just to the left of you is a gate. Go through this onto a green track, descending, with a wall on the left. To the right the nearest high point on the fell is Wansfell Pike.

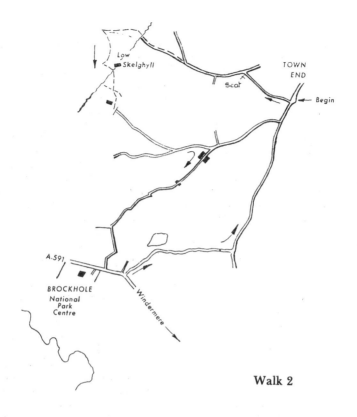

Walk 2

Views of the fells, left, are of Wetherlam, Crinkle Crags, Bowfell and Langdale Pikes. Wray Castle can be seen in the wood by the lake shore, Blelham Tarn above it.

Go through the gate, avoiding the wetness as best you may. The track curves to cross a beck, then goes through two old gateways and past a ruined barn. At this point the track becomes a green footpath across a field. Curve left with it and descend the hill. Soon it finishes at the foot of a wall on the bank of a ghyll. Go through the wicket gate, but do not cross the bridge. Turn immediately left and go through the gate and onto another hard track. Go through gate and down the zig-zag to Low Skelghyll. Go through the gate and past the buildings. After this a barn is reached and the lane bends left to go through an iron gate. After a while a public road is approached, but near the end of your lane examine the stump of a felled ash tree. Its age can be calculated by counting the annual rings from the centre; as a new ring is made every year of growth it seems to be well over a hundred years old.

13

When the road is joined go up to the left. A large barn, with another one behind it, will soon be seen, on the right. Take the track, right, which goes between these barns, and descends. This is again a walled track, on stony ground. After a ruined barn the track becomes green. There are views again left over Windermere, and a little tarn below left, which you will pass on the return journey. Go through a gate, by a large sycamore. From this point on, tree admirers will see some good specimens. The path descends towards some buildings, between a large beech tree and another large sycamore. There are two gates ahead. Go through the left-hand one. Go onto a macadam lane for a few yards before turning right over a little beck and onto a green track, which changes to a stony track and rises. There is an old oak tree over wall to left. Eventually the track descends and curves off left with the wall. It falls to a hard surfaced lane among buildings. Continue on. In the fields of the estate hereabouts, thoroughbred ponies are bred, and carefully raised and fed. The owners understandably do not like passers-by to feed them, even though the ponies may ask. Conversation with them and photograph-taking is, however, allowed. The main road is joined. Cross it with great care. Brockhole is on the far side of the road to the right.

On leaving Brockhole turn right and continue along pavement. Soon the road curves to the right. If you look at the opposite side of the road you will see two entrances. You take the one on the right, on a well-defined green lane. Cross the beck soon by slate footbridge. Only tall people can see the tarn over the wall on the left. However as you progress the wall finishes and the track bears left to give views over the tarn. There are usually ducks in residence. Now the track begins to climb. And climb. Rest when the walls open up to a green area and look back at the lake. Eventually the track levels off and the public road is joined. Turn right, and your car is a little way up the road.

4 miles [6.5 km]

O.S. 1:50,000 Sheet No. 90

This walk gives the best views over Rydal Water and takes one to the man-made caves of Loughrigg Quarry. Wordsworth enthusiasts can visit Rydal Mount, the home of the poet for thirty-seven years. The walk has the merit that, with luck, one can arrive back with reasonably dry footwear; but timid females will have to have a hand over the Rothay stepping stones, which are in fact quite safe but should not be attempted in flood conditions.

Park the car on one of the Ambleside car parks. Walk on along main road towards Grasmere and Keswick. The curious Bridge House is passed. Its origin is something of a mystery but one theory is that it was built by someone to avoid paying land rent. It is now an information centre of the National Trust. Somewhere near the Police Station cross over to right hand side of road. When the pavement ends at a drive entrance cross the road again with great care. After half a mile the cricket field is on the left, and after this there is a wood above the road level. At the end of this wood there is a gate into a field. Go through the gate, and obviously it must be very firmly fastened behind you.

There is no apparent path in the field, but slightly to right of front, beyond a slight knoll, is a group of trees. Head for the right of these. There is no access-right to this field and you may not stop to picnic or play games; there is only a right of way across it. Continue past the trees on the same line and the river will be reached and the stepping stones. Cross these with care to join road at the other side. Turn right. Go through the gate by the cattle grid and continue along the road to another gate and cattle grid. Turn left down the lane through another. Follow this lane until an iron gate is reached which leads onto fell land and distinct tracks. Take the upper track, and at the seat there is a perfect view over Rydal Water. The crags across the lake are Nab Scar. The cottage at the foot was the home of Hartley Coleridge, son of Samuel Taylor Coleridge and friend of the Wordsworths.

Follow the track up, through woodland. After a bend right a conical crag will be seen and Loughrigg Quarry has been reached. If we go to the left of this crag the smallest cave will be seen across a gully. Go back onto the track and continue up, zig-zagging left then right through some attractive larch trees. The big cave can then be seen and entered.

The platform of waste opposite the cave entrance is a natural rock garden and stonecrop proliferates. (Please do not uproot!) Although there is little soil here, if the land was not grazed by sheep

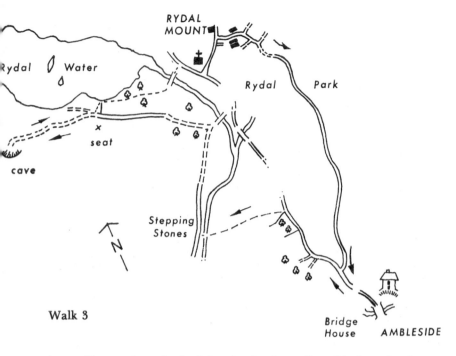

RYDAL MOUNT

Rydal Water

Rydal Park

cave

seat

Stepping Stones

N

Walk 3

Bridge House   AMBLESIDE

it would soon be colonised by the larches, silver birch and ash trees which can all take root in the quarry waste. Where sheep cannot reach seeds will germinate. A tiny birch tree can be seen growing in a crack above the cave entrance.

Follow the track back to the view-point seat, then descend towards lake and a kissing-gate will be seen in the wall on the right. Go through this into the wood. Follow it to a footbridge. This brings us onto the main road again. Cross it with great care. Turn right towards Ambleside but go left up the nearby access road. Rydal Chapel is on the left. Wordsworth helped to choose the site where it was built and worshipped here regularly. If it is daffodil season then we must go through the chapel yard to Dora's Field beyond, to see a golden carpet.

Go on up the road. Some old cottages can be seen on the left. Just above them is Rydal Mount which is now open to the public. Our way from here is on the right. Just above the entrance drive to Rydal Hall, which is a conference centre and not open to the public, there is another entrance onto a lane. Follow this through the yards of the buildings, turning right at the end after crossing the bridge, then bearing left at the Y junction. Across the green ahead there are some fine tall Noble Firs. Follow the hard track by some fine

16

specimen trees. Some of them are labelled. A large sitka spruce can be seen close to the track, and those who have done the Claife walks and seen the young sitkas there might marvel at the difference.

This is Rydal Park. It is the private park of Rydal Hall and there is no access off the lane but we can enjoy the walk along this pleasant lane none the less. There are some fine trees and the well cared-for fields can be an unbelievably bright green. They are the scene of the well known Rydal Sheep Dog Trials.

The main road is joined again through some tall iron gates. Cross the road to the pavement on the far side *with great care*. Continue left to Ambleside, about a third of a mile.

There was a time when it was possible to walk up the main road in Great Langdale and enjoy its contrasting views of lush green valley and sharp crag sides in tranquillity. If one tried it now there would be too much dodging from the traffic, for safety, to enjoy anything. The safest way to proceed up the valley's main route is in one's own steel box on wheels. But so much is missed in the haste. And one can hardly stop to take something in before someone is hooting from behind.

But there is another way up the valley on a parallel route. And being more central in its situation the view up valley is far superior. Furthermore, the odds are that you will find the route quiet and hardly used. The return journey is a woodland walk.

Park your car in Elterwater village, or if congestion prevents this, on the common. Walk to the bridge in the village and cross it. Immediately on the other side, to the right, a road follows the beck upstream. This is a road to the quarries and is probably marked 'Private'. Ignore the sign. It means that no vehicles can proceed. There is a right of way on foot and no-one can legally prevent passage. As you walk along the road you will see on the opposite bank a complex of buildings and waterways. Most of this is now holiday accommodation though it was formerly a thriving gunpowder works. The making of gunpowder was once a thriving Lake District industry. The works opened in 1824 and produced 4,000 to 6,000 pounds of the powder per week and was in full production in the First World War until 1918.

Presently you will see that the old quarry workings cut into the hillside on the left. There is a large tunnel sealed off with corrugated iron and warning notices — and the way leaves the road here, on the opposite side, down a green track to the beck bank. Follow the river bank past the weir with the old quarry waste heaps on the left. Presently a long wooden footbridge will be reached. Cross it and join road; but only for a little way. Turn left and the village of Chapel Stile is before you but ignore it by turning left up a track just past the Langdales Hotel. (Public conveniences opposite.) This changes for a short stretch into a road with the village school in the trees to the right, and the graveyard on the left, a simple green field with only an ornate gate and exotic shrubs to distinguish it from any other field. Do not follow road right but continue on past the buildings, Thrang. Go through narrow gate and down green track between walls. This joins a hard-core lane; bear left and cross the bridge.

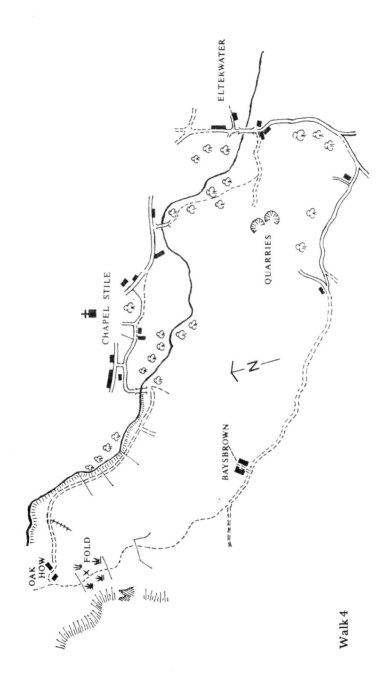

ELTERWATER

CHAPEL STILE

QUARRIES

OAK
HOW

FOLD

BAYSBROWN

N

Walk 4

(A stone in the parapet is marked 'Built 1818. John & Jane Atkinson.') The path crosses a rock slab and follows beck-bank right. After half a mile the view of the valley head opens up. There are several gates. If they are open, leave them open. If they are closed, close them after you. At this point where the track leaves the bank slightly, there is probably the best view of Langdale Pikes. This is the place for an artist to set up his easel. Ahead to the left the old farm dwelling of Oak How is dwarfed by the large Scots Pines and the yew tree. It could only belong where it is.

The track eventually curves off towards Oak How, and keen map readers with the one-inch Ordnance Survey tourist map might note that this is now a public road which also goes right, across a ford to Harry Place. But the River Board have dredged it away and built up the banks so that anyone who wishes to assert his rights to pass along a highway could easily be drowned. (Legal experts might advise the author if the dependants could then claim damages from the Highway Authority.) But left to Oak How, and beyond it the way bends left, and from here we go back down the valley. It is wet here, and young ladies who have taken ballet lessons might be at an advantage, as bog avoidance means dancing from stone to stone.

Go through gate and keep wall to the left. The large crags above on the right are Oak How Crags, the eastern face of Lingmoor Fell. Spare time from bog-dodging to look back at these crags after about half a mile, and it will be seen that a jagged section of the crag is detached from the rest. This is called 'Oak How Needle'. Presently there is a sheep fold left, apparently made from an old barn, and below it in the field, a detached crag with large trees growing out of it. Through gate, as we proceed, there is a smooth glaciated slab of green slate. A wood is now entered, and there is more wetness to avoid. The green track eventually ends on a hard road to the quarries above. Go left down hill towards the farm of Baysbrown. The front wall of this farm is faced with green slate. Continue on, bearing right and upwards into another wood. The roadsides here are littered with green slate fragments. The wood at first is mostly hardwood with much hazel coppice, but this changes to conifer woodland gradually until a house is reached after half a mile. Continue on, take a last look at the Pikes over a sea of silver birch.

The road drops between walls covered with miniature rock gardens. (Please do not attempt to uproot the ferns!) Continue directly down until another rough road is joined, after passing a barn on the left. Turn left along this road, and after a short distance the macadam road is reached. Turn left, back into the village of Elterwater.

O.S. 1:50,000 Sheet No. 90

This is a very varied walk through woodlands and fields, taking in a tarn, a green-slate mill, a waterfall and a small lake, with some excellent views. It nearly has everything, so that although the walk could take only a leisurely 2½ hours, extra should be added if you take photographs, or are interested in the Lakeland slate industry.

The walk starts at Elterwater Common. From Ambleside take the Coniston/Langdale road. After 2¾ miles take the branch road, right, for Langdale. The open common is reached after one mile, and there are ample parking spaces.

Walk back the way you have driven until you come to the first branch road on the left. Turn left up it. This is a public road, but a quiet one. It climbs gently through woodland. Ignore the junction with road from the right, and continue on to the T junction. Turn round just before you reach it, for a view of the Coniston Old Man range's northern flank, with Wetherlam nearest, then Swirl How and Grey Friar.

Take the right turn at the T junction, and after two minutes' walk the road widens on the left revealing a gate there. Take the path which goes from it towards the tarn. After the gate you go towards the corner of the old hedge, bear right slightly, then left through another gate. Then go forward to ascend to the lane, through a gate between the beech trees and the oak. Turn right. Just along here is one of the best views of the tarn, framed by trees, with Wetherlam in the background. Further on, round the corner, is another fine view, this time backed by the Langdale Pikes.

The lane leaves the tarn now and on the left, unless old age strikes it down, there is a large birch tree with unusually prolific examples of the peculiar twig growths known as 'witch's broom', looking like so many bird's nests. This is caused by a fungus. Bear right at junction near the buildings, then left to join macadam road. Turn right, and almost immediately leave the road, left, to descend the lane which goes past the entrance to the Neaum Crag National Park camp site. This lane finishes at the Langdale road, near to its junction with the Coniston road near Skelwith Bridge. Cross the Langdale road, and pass the front of the Skelwith Bridge Hotel. Walk to the bridge. This is a two-span structure across the river Brathay, which was the boundary between Westmorland, on your side, and Lancashire on the far side. Do not cross the bridge but continue on with the river on your left. This goes by the showroom of the Kirkstone Green Slate Quarry Company, which is worth a visit. The Lake District slate is exported all over the world. The way goes

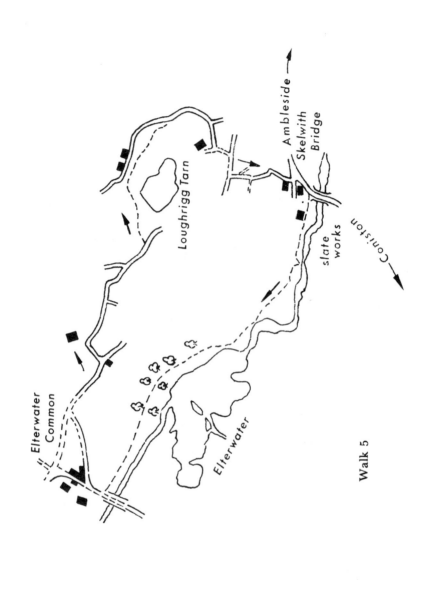

Elterwater Common

Loughrigg Tarn

Elterwater

Ambleside

Skelwith
Bridge

slate
works

Coniston

Walk 5

right through the company's mill yard, usually past large blocks of slate waiting to be cut. The special saw, set with diamond teeth which cut the slate, is in the shed on the left. Do not assume that odd pieces of green slate lying about are just waste. It is nearly all saleable, and if you wish to buy a piece call at the office!

The path is then alongside the river, and goes by the waterfall, 'Skelwith Force' as it is called; 'force' being the local name for a waterfall. It is a short, pounding fall, especially impressive after heavy rain. It can be viewed by crossing the wooden bridge, and then the steel one below that. Take care if wetness makes the way slippery.

The path onward then goes up and through a gate into a field. Head across, aiming to the right of the woody knoll, then bear right for a footbridge across very muddy ground. It is approached by a stone causeway. The narrow gateway beyond is very muddy, but the worst can be avoided by turning right immediately through it, follow the wall for a short way, then turn left again across stepping stones to the other side of the mud patch. Follow the river bank round. The river is quite deep and clear, close to the bank at its normal course. Just before reaching the stone wall there is a fine view, a photographer's dream of a view if the light is right, out across Elterwater to the Langdale Pikes.

Go through the kissing gate. (Why is this sort of gate called so? Because it offers lovers opportunity for embracing? Or because the gate 'kisses' the fence on either side?) The way then passes through pleasant woods with glimpses of the lake, then eventually leaves them through another kissing-gate. Go on directly across the field path, through a wall gap, and on to a gate at the left of a large oak tree. Follow the grass track which finishes eventually by the bridge at Elterwater village. Turn right, go as signposted 'Grasmere, Ambleside' and the road brings you to Elterwater Common, the starting point.

O.S. 1:50,000 Sheet No. 90

This is a modest climb, but it makes a very pleasant walk. The best time to view any waterfall is after heavy rain. The walk goes by the well-known force (local-name for waterfall), climbs beyond it, and returns through farm fields. (If dogs are taken they should be kept firmly under control.)

Start at Ambleside and cross in the square, after having parked your car in one of the village car parks. On the eastern side of the square is the Salutation Hotel (the 'Sally'). Next to this is a bank. Between this bank and the old market hall is a passageway. Go up this. Turn left up the hill, and along an access road. There is an old mill beyond the ghyll left, now converted into holiday flats. Bear left through gateway and along the track which follows the ghyll. This land is managed by the local council as a public access area. When track forks, continue right on higher level. After ascending rock steps, on another few yards, then, ascending two steps of oak roots, turn left over the rock to the iron fence. Go through the iron arches to the viewpoints. Return the same way through the arches, then turn left to another viewpoint. Return to path and continue to climb. Follow the iron fence. There are good views at the fence corners. Go up rough stone steps and onto footbridge, for the down views.

Follow the path back. When it divides after slate bridges take left fork, and follow this track to a turnstile; a Victorian relic which ought to be preserved! Turn left at the track beyond and go up the hill and through the gate. You are now out of the wood. The Kirkstone Road via the 'Struggle' can be seen on the left, and the heights of Red Screes, above Kirkstone, are at the head of the valley. Wansfell is the fell on the right. Go through the gate. The track is crossed by a beck and a second beck is crossed by a little footbridge with stiles. Turn left after the barn and go down to the plank bridge at the ghyll below. Turn left. Track turns with the wall, but instead of continuing right, up the hill, go through the stile in the wall, alongside the gate. Make towards the barn forward and right. Go over the stone step-stile beside the gate near this barn. (This is a bit awkward. Ladies will require help.) Path follows the wall and an old hedge. Go through gateway. (Close gate if you find it closed on approach.) Continue following old hedge and then a wall. View ahead from Wetherlam left. Langdale Pikes are off to the right. Go through the stile by the cottage. There is another stile by the gate just beyond it. Continue down a good hard-surfaced track. Iron wicket gates to right and left just below this mark the right of way for the North-West Water Authority inspectors, for the pipe from

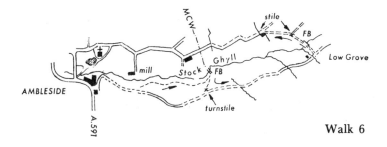

Thirlmere passes under this point. The way becomes an access road. Langdale Pikes have now been moved. They are ahead!

The track meets the public road. Join it with care and go left down the hill. A pavement is picked up lower down. It ends by a road into an estate. Beyond this is the entrance to the Kirkstone Foot Hotel. Bear left past this entrance and go down the hill with the church on the right. At the square turn left down Peggy Hill which brings you to the cross again.

3 miles [5 km]

O.S. 1:50,000 Sheet No. 90

This is a very minor fell walk onto the south-eastern crags of Loughrigg. Given time, it can be managed by grannies and children. It is however, *not* a bad-weather walk. The walk offers airy views; so little satisfaction is gained if rain or mist restricts visibility. Completely smooth-soled footwear is a danger on the damp rock that is found on the walk, or on dry sloping grass if the walk is done in a heat-wave.

Park the car in an Ambleside car park. Go to the spired parish church of St Mary to start the walk. Go through the churchyard main gate and at the far end turn left and go through the iron gate and into the park (Rothay Park). Go straight ahead down the path. This ends in a small footbridge which is followed by a large arched bridge called Miller Bridge, typical of the Lake District. Cross it to join road and turn right for a few yards, go through the gate alongside the cattle grid, then turn left at the drive and go through the gate alongside that cattle grid. Go right up the curving drive. Note the old slate fence on the left. These are commoner in the Hawkshead area. At the top of the drive, after going through the gate, bear left for the wall corner surmounted by the iron ladder-stile. From the stile the path turns left by a fence under a handsome Scots Pine. Go through the slate stile, cross the small stream and go directly upwards on the path. Looking back (for a breather?) at first level of this path by the oak trees over our pine tree, there is a fine view over Rydal which runs up to the head of Fairfield (2,863 feet high). The valley to its right is Scandale, and to the right of that is the Stock Ghyll ascent to Kirkstone Pass, the Lake District's highest road pass — the 'Struggle' being near the top of it.

Continue straight on across another beck, joining the path that comes up from the left. Continue up to a cairn. There is now a good view of Ambleside, looking like a toy village, and there is a view of the upper reaches of Windermere. Continue on past the cairn, down the dip and up the rise to the crags. Now here is a good view down the lake. The river Rothay flows in from the left by Ambleside. The tarn in the hills, right front, is Blelham Tarn, a nature reserve. Beyond the point where the river flows into the lake, the square foundations of the Roman fort known as Galava can be seen in the field.

Continue on along the path to a wooden ladder stile, and up the next crag. Leave this crag by descending it on its lake side, then bearing right. Below, the river Brathay can be seen coming from the right from the Langdales, to join the Rothay before entering

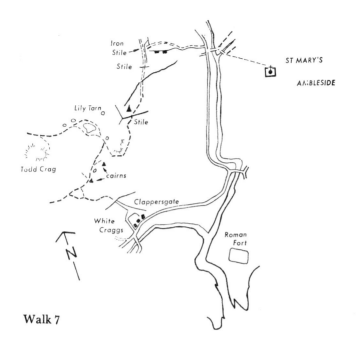

Walk 7

Windermere. Go onto the next crag. And here is the place to relax and enjoy the scene. Looking at the high fells on view to the right, the first from the left is the large hump of Wetherlam, then Swirl How and Grey Friar, all these on the Coniston Old Man range. The nearer fell then is Lingmoor, with the pack just over its left shoulder — Pike o' Blisco. The distant peak then is the point of Bowfell, which looks like a mountain from any angle. To the right again, but nearer, are the unmistakable Langdale Pikes with the great crag of Pavey Ark attached to the right. (You may see climbers on this if you have binoculars.) To right again are the Wythburn Fells, the dip of Dunmail Raise, then Seat Sandal stands before the Helvellyn range. Then to right of that the Fairfield Horseshoe in its impressive folds.

Are we standing on Todd Crag? Some say that this is in fact Todd Crag, including Wainwright who wrote the famous Fell Guides. But the gentlemen of the Ordnance Survey put it further west. The point on which you stand offers the best view, in my opinion, but to settle the argument it is only a few minutes to the 'official' Todd Crag.

Turn your back on the Lake view and below you will see a pond. Descend to it, and continue on the path which leads beyond it on its left. This brings you to Lily Tarn. This indeed bears water lilies in their season. They are not unusally picked by the selfish few whose reaction to seeing anything pretty is 'I want'. Pickers can be fined under the National Trust bye-laws, but are seldom caught. The tarn is particularly beautiful if it reflects a blue sky.

Take the path to its right and go round the tarn to its far side to a path going slightly left, and on slightly left of two small ponds.

When this joins a wall running on its left, go forward until there is a gap in the wall and go through it. Of the two crags before you the one on the right has been officially labelled as Todd Crag. It looks a feeble little crag in a grassy area, but the crag proper is before and below you, invisible from this point, and clothed with trees. The better view point is from the crag on the left. Looking back one can see that Loughrigg has many peaks, and though the highest point is only 1,100 feet it is a very large mass. It is the easiest thing in the world to get lost on Loughrigg. But not for us. Retrace steps down the way of arrival, to the wall gap, and right, then bearing slightly left to the little ponds and Lily Tarn. Remember that we have to go right round the Tarn and down to the first pond, but then, having reached it, bear right by the path towards a cairn at the foot of our earlier viewpoint crag, then continue right by the footpath which begins the descent. There is another cairn on the site of a ruined hut, and a path from the right joins. Descend. The zig-zag towards the wall is easier going; then keep on descending left along an airy path by gorse and mountain ash, under an oak and birch-clad crag. Go through gate and bear down right. There is an attractive dead-oak 'sculpture' on the left.

The path soon brings us on to the roadside (the Ambleside to Langdale and Coniston road, with the branch road ahead to Hawkshead). If you have time, a visit to White Crags, a wonderful garden open to the public, is a 'must' as it is only a few yards on the right. It is at its best in late May and June, but there is always something to see. Turn right, and just past the corner of the building you will see White Crags' drive bearing off to the right.

To return to our starting point then, turn left past the few buildings that make up this tiny hamlet of Clappersgate. At the end of the few cottages, cross over the road with care, to the far sidewalk. Continue towards Ambleside, but just before the bridge (Rothay Bridge) cross the road again with great care, and go up the narrow road opposite. Follow this for about a third of a mile and we are back at Miller Bridge, which we cross again to go through the park to the church.

O.S. 1:50,000 Sheet No. 90

This is a short walk which can fill in a very pleasant hour or more. It is routed most of the way over hard-surfaced tracks and one has a very reasonable chance of returning dry-shod. (Some children excepted, who could find mud in the Sahara.) A man with reasonable lungs could push a perambulator along it!

The walk starts at a lane junction with the Ambleside to Coniston road. From Ambleside take the Coniston junction at Skelwith Bridge and continue for about 1¾ miles. The lane is on the right at the top of the hill, and is the one after the road which is signposted 'Wrynose Pass, Elterwater, Little Langdale'. At the time of writing this lane is merely signposted 'Unfit for Cars'. Turning in at this lane there is immediately a grass area on the left with space for parking. From Coniston the lane is about four miles along the Ambleside road, beyond the hill crest and beginning the descent.

Having parked, take the right-hand road. A plantation of spruce and larch and Scots Pine is on the right. Shortly the bulk of Wetherlam can be seen on the left. Then there is a craggy outcrop in the field on the left, and through the gap can be seen Lingmoor. The protuberance is Busk Pike. There are soon some handsome Scots Pine, right. The crag on the left is Little Fell. The road begins to fall and the view of the fells open up, towards the north. The mountain on the left is the Helvellyn range; then there is the gap of Grisedale Hause; then the Fairfield range with the highest point at the rear, and the peaks of Greatrigg, and Heron Pike before; to the right of that is the valley head of Rydal, then the peaks of Hart Crag and Dove Crag; the nearest and lower fell is Loughrigg, with Elterwater below it. As you turn a corner, go through the gate, and there is a view of the lower part of Little Langdale. The buildings of High Park, typical old dwellings in the care of the National Trust, are now approached. Continue along the road and the buildings of Stang End are reached. At Stang End turn left and up the hill past the barn where the road surface changes to stone.

The road winds and climbs between birch woods. The views to the right are of Pike o'Blisco; behind is Crinkle Crags; and to the right the impressive hump of Bowfell. The quarries of Moss Rigg are seen. The tree-clothed crag on the left makes a pretty picture. Go through a gate and continue on the stony track, which changes to macadam as it goes through mixed woodlands. Ignore branch road to the right. Some quarry buildings are approached. The old quarry heaps have been taken over by silver birch trees which are self-seeded. They are invariably the first trees to colonise the sparse

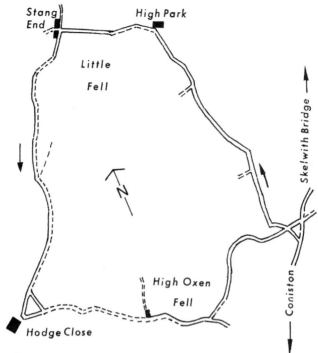

Walk 8

pockets of soil, their leaf mould later giving other species an opportunity to join them. There are cottages on the right. This is Hodge Close. Very shortly after this there is a very sharp turning to the left, a stone track, with a slate supporting wall on its right containing the quarry waste from above. Take this track. At the top of the first rise there is a little reedy pool on the left. The track rises and falls, then passes through a gate.

You are now on a piece of fell land among juniper bushes. The berries of the juniper have long been used as a valuable herb for kidney ailments but are more commonly known for their vital job of flavouring gin. The green berries have the sharp gin taste, the ripe black berries are too sweet and sickly. The bush, looking like a cross between gorse and a miniature yew tree, is common on the Lake District fells. It is our only native member of the cypress family, and is getting scarcer in some parts of Britain. The track zig-zags, then culverts a beck, then goes through the farmyard of High Oxen Fell, where the surface changes again to macadam. It rises and there are fine views to the left. At the fork bear left. The road falls to Low Oxen Fell Falls, to cross a beck, then rises slightly and you are soon back at the crossroads where the car is parked.

This is a woodland walk on clearly seen tracks, half of the distance being done on the lake shore. Seekers after peace and quiet may find Windermere's shore less pleasant on Sundays in the season when motor-boats are in full flight. Otherwise this is a walk for all seasons. In winter, quiet folk without boisterous dogs have a good chance of seeing wild deer.

The walk starts at Wray Castle, a monument to Victorian romantic nonsense on the shores of Windermere, and in the care of the National Trust. It is reached from Ambleside by taking the Coniston/Langdales road; turning left for Hawkshead and left again for Wray. In fact, after leaving on the Coniston road it is a series of left turns for two miles, and when the road climbs and turns right, the castle gates are seen on the left. From Coniston it is via Hawkshead. From Hawkshead take the Windermere Ferry road and take the first turn left signposted Wray, 2½ miles. Drive through the gates and down the drive to the castle. The car park is just beyond the building. The story has it that the man who had the castle built, together with some mock ruins which have been demolished in the interests of public safety, presented it as a surprise home for his wife. She took one look at it, shuddered, and said that if it was all the same to him she would like to return to her less extravagant quarters, and she would rather like to go at once as she had just remembered that her library books were overdue! There are some handsome trees in the 64 acres of grounds, including a mulberry planted by William Wordsworth himself, alongside an unusual fern-leafed beech.

After parking the car, walk back down the drive and leave by the gateway into the road and turn left. Cut the corner of the second bend on, by following the path on the grass to the right, alongside the fence. As we climb on up to the small hamlet of High Wray there is a view of a stretch of Windermere left. Go right through the hamlet. Ignore the branch road left. Just after this branch road there is a cottage, and a few yards beyond that a cattle-grid in a gateway to the left. Go over this. (Signposted 'Ferry' if the vandals have spared it.) Go up this track, and as you gain height look back at the good view of the lake ahead and Ambleside. The buildings of Base Camp can soon be seen on the left.

Base Camp is a camp site owned by the National Trust, offered inexpensively to organised youth groups on the understanding that they will give a certain amount of work to the Trust or to a local project. Go over the stile at the gateway and wind up the hill. We

31

soon enter the Forestry Commission's plantations. It might be inadvisable to mention tree species in the Commission's lands as by the time this is read the planting pattern may have changed. But at the time of writing there are sitka spruces planted left, and on the right there is a mixture of larches and Norway spruces. Larches are bare of needles in winter, and in summer they are a lighter green than the dark spruces. As the forest road levels out at the top of the hill there are more mature woodlands; young Japanese larch on the left, sitka spruce on right; and as the road descends a little there are Japanese larch all around. This tree can be distinguished from the European variety by its pinkish twigs, European larch being straw coloured. Japanese larch grows more quickly.

Presently the forest road forks. Take the left-hand road. As you descend here there is a good view up the Troutbeck valley across the lake with the High Street walling it in behind. On the left in several places, at least at the time of writing this, there are areas of spruce badly damaged by deer grazing. One or two trees may be seen that have been 'frayed' by roe deer. Roe-bucks mark their territory by rubbing their antlers on young trees which damages the trees by scraping off the bark. You presently reach a crossroads — a meeting of five paths and tracks. Take the first turning left, which doubles sharply back. This track is wet in places and diversions may be necessary on surrounding banks. A beck has to be crossed — easy except after heavy rain. The Forestry Commission land is left through a gate and you are at a National Trust wood. Descend track through maturer wood of European Larch and Douglas Firs. This track was once an important route to Hawkshead and was paved and well kept, but time, neglect and the extraction of timber have been its ruin.

As you near the lower levels of this track the woodland is more typical — oaks, birches and yew. The walls of Belle Grange can soon be seen below. On reaching, follow the wall down to its bottom where a track T junction will be found. (Note distinctive Scots Pine over the wall). Turn left and you are soon walking along a lake shore track. Stand on a promontory of shingle a little way along, by an old gateway and where a beck enters the lake, for there is a view across the lake to Adelaide Hill on the right, the green one; a well-known view north of Bowness and west of Windermere. Straight ahead is Calgarth, an old mansion. Troutbeck is behind. From the same point, but on the other side of the beck, is a good view up the lake; Ambleside scattered about the head. Across the lake, right, the cream-coloured building is Brockhole, the National Park Centre.

After a second old gateway the track forks. The left-hand one is macadam. We take the right-hand one which continues along the lake shore. There is now coppiced woodland on the left. Hardwoods were once continually 'coppiced' to produce a regular supply of

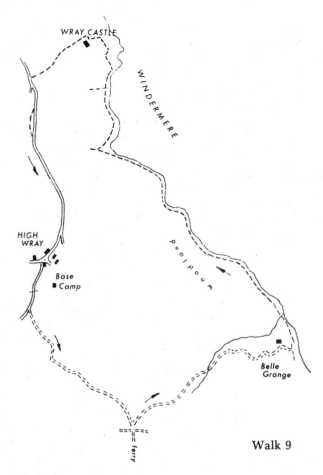

WRAY CASTLE

WINDERMERE

HIGH
WRAY

Base
■ Camp

Pull Wood

Belle
Grange

ferry

Walk 9

timber. That is, the trees were felled, new stems grew up from the stump or 'stool', and after twelve years or so these stems had grown sufficiently to harvest. In another twelve years or more another crop would have grown; and so the process continued. Now the price of coppice wood is so depressed that it is hardly worth the labour costs of felling. Some single stems of oak have been allowed to develop into maturity on the lake side of the track. The thickest growth along the track side is of hazel, which thrives in these lower areas. Red squirrels (there are to date no grey squirrels in the Lake District; for which we should be grateful as they are destructive) thrive on the nuts. A lot of the hazel is intertwined with honeysuckle. If you find any in bloom please leave it for others to enjoy. The

33

by-laws here protect wild plants, and one can be fined for taking them. The path eventually skirts a little bay called High Wray Bay. Go through the gate and continue on lake shore. At the next gate, go through stile alongside it, and go up the lane away from the lake for about forty yards, then on the right there is a gap in the wall and a stile. Go over this, and join the lake shore again by the boat house. There is no path here now we are on an open field, but you are in Wray Castle grounds and can walk by the lake. Unless the lake is high, it is possible to walk along the shingle beach. Where the way is barred by a fence, go a little way up it and through the wicket gate Follow the lake shore again to the next fence then follow it upwards by the stepped zig-zag. The castle is now ahead. But between you and it is the boy-scout camping field. If there are tents there, it would be a discourtesy to walk through them. Go instead through the iron gate on your right, then follow the path on left, on the other side of the fence, which climbs a little knoll. Note the odd shape of the large Douglas Firs in the field. The castle is approached through the stone fence posts of an old wicket gate.

O.S. 1:50,000 Sheet No. 90

The title of this walk may sound formidable. In fact Black Crag is a little hump of rock on a softly-contoured fell south of Skelwith Bridge. The Mountain Road is the local name for a hard track at a modest level, north of Tarn Hows. However, for anyone who has not stretched his legs at other walks in this book, the journey might be somewhat heroic! But this walk should not be done in mist, as good views are its fine feature. Part of the way is muddy. Having said that, the walk is delightful, and an adventure.

From Ambleside take the Coniston Road, continuing as for Coniston at the junction with the Langdale road at Skelwith Bridge for about 1¾ miles. At the top of the long hill take the second turning right; that is the one after the road signposted 'Wrynose'. At the time of writing the road you want is signposted 'Unfit for Cars'. Pull in on this road, and park on the grassed area just inside. From Coniston the road above is four miles along the Ambleside road, beyond the hill crest and beginning the descent. The starting point is the same as for Walk 8.

After parking, return to the main Ambleside to Coniston road and cross it. Go up the grass track, past the seat, which is opposite. Go through gate and on along track, avoiding wetness by higher ground right if necessary. The mixed woodlands away to the left are very colourful in spring and autumn. After crossing a little beck, turn right across a wet area to follow the wall which is on the left, but at some distance from it. A hundred yards up, the track is better seen and is on drier ground, as it zig-zags up the hill. Looking back as you climb there is a view of Elterwater. Near the top the track bears left through a gate. Here it is more difficult to see, but it follows the wall which is now on the right. Go through gate towards the buildings of Low Arnside Farm, hidden among trees. Bear left just before the farm, up a more distinct stony track. The track meanders, then goes through a gateway, and follows a wall which is on the right. On approaching the crown of the hill there is another gateway. Just beyond this the track levels, and there is a large bog on the left. Turn off this track here. Just before the bog, a track will be seen bearing sharply left round a rocky knoll. This is your way. Unfortunately the old track here has been drowned in the bog, but it is possible to pick it up by skirting the knoll, and following close to the wall on the left across stepping stones. The good built-up track is then picked up following the wall upwards. Following this track and looking left at Low Arnside one can see how the old Lake District farms were built—backs to the wind in a sheltered

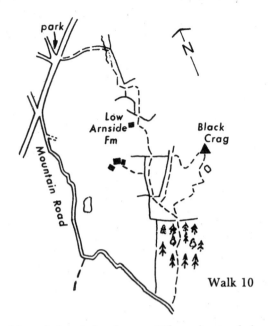

park

Low
Arnside
Fm

Black
Crag

Mountain Road

Walk 10

hollow, with a shelter-belt of trees. When the track begins to fall it is time to leave it. To find the point recommended; over the wall to the left another wall can be seen coming up to join it. It is just before this joining. At the foot of your wall following the track can be seen a 'hog-hole'. (Hog is a yearling sheep.) This is a little passage way for sheep. Strike up the bank immediately opposite to this. On reaching the top of the first rise, the square-looking cairn on the knobbly top of Black Crag can be seen ahead. This is the point to be eventually reached. To avoid bog and unnecessary loss of height, do not go straight ahead towards it, but bear right towards where the top of a larch tree can be seen above the brow of a hill. Go by this tree and cross the wet ground below it; cross the rising ground to the right, cross the wet ground beyond that, and walk up to the track which crosses your view ahead. Go right across this green track and toil up the hill.

The ground now is rough; take the ascent to the left, using the grass as much as possible in preference to loose rock. You will then arrive at the Ordnance Survey's triangulation pillar on the summit; possibly if you have rushed it, in a near state of collapse! The pillar has the unusual distinction of bearing a National Trust emblem. The view over Windermere is a delightful surprise. Blelham Tarn can be seen below; then right, Esthwaite Water and nearer, Tarn Hows. Above Tarn Hows you should see Coniston Water. The fell views, visibility allowing, are remarkable. As always in this area the Coniston Old Man range dominates the scene, left, if you face the

36

way you have come. The knobbly crags to the right and farther back are Crinkle Crags; just forward of these and a little right is the pointed peak of Pike o'Blisco, and between it and the large hump of the next mountain, Bowfell, might be seen the distant tip of Scafell Pike, the highest point in England (3,206 feet according to the Ordnance Survey's last measurement; it seems to have lost four feet since previous counts). On the other side of Bowfell is Great End, the northern hump of the Scafell Pikes range. Then there are the Langdale Pikes curved, right, with the great crag face of Pavey Arc. Then there are the softer shapes, but high fells, of High Raise and Ullscarf, and a little nearer, Steel Fell. The gap of Dunmail Raise is next, and through it, if visibility is specially good, there is the distant rise of 'Saddleback' or Blencathra. The Helvellyn range is then seen end-on, the summit point almost at due north. Nearer and to right is the Fairfield range, followed by the gap of Kirkstone Pass, then there is the High Street range.

After enjoying the view, descend a little way by the same route as that by which you arrived, then incline left, towards Tarn Hows. A path should then be picked up which passes by a little pool. After passing the pool the path bears left a little, and after crossing a small gully it bends left round a little crag outcrop. Although this is only a footpath it should be clearly seen. It meanders and rises and falls, and heads in the general direction of Tarn Hows. It eventually joins a track.

Turn left along the track, go through a gateway and alongside a dense spruce wood. On approaching wood ahead keep close to left-hand wall to avoid bog. Go through the gate or over the stile into the plantation. Go directly on down the track. It is probably wet at first, but it improves on the descent. The plantation is largely of Japanese Larch, broken up by spruce, and with one or two older and oddly shaped European Larch. Leave the plantation at the bottom by the gate or stile. Follow the track down, through an old gateway and you are onto the Mountain Road. Turn right.

Those who had difficulty in the largely trackless area of Black Crag need be assured now that one would have to try very hard to get lost. The road is well made, fenced both sides, and raised above the bogs. Presently there is a view of Tarn Hows on the left. Later there is a little tarn on the right. The mile or so walk on this road is a delight. It eventually, however, falls to join the main Ambleside to Coniston road again. Go directly, and with care, over the road, and enter through the gateway into the lane opposite. However, immediately through this gateway turn right and follow the wall through the pine trees, cross the wooden footbridge and go over the ladder stile. Then continue alongside the wall along the field. This is a path, provided by the National Trust, to keep pedestrians off the narrow road alongside. If we follow the path along the wall another ladder stile is reached, and on climbing it you are back at the starting point.

Grasmere is Wordsworth country for it was here, at Dove Cottage, that he wrote his best, and nearby he lived until his death. This walk is the classic walk of the Lake District. No lover of Wordsworth can miss it. Every lover of the Lake District must do it at least once. Because it is so popular no one who wants to wander 'lonely as a cloud' will attempt it on a bank holiday. If you are calling at Dove Cottage, which is on the route, be warned that the cottage is closed on Sundays. Allow two and a half hours for the walk—but much longer if you want to lounge with a view across the lake, or linger at Grasmere church, Dove Cottage or the Wordsworth Museum.

The walk starts at Whitemoss Common. This is a mile south of Grasmere on the Ambleside road. From Ambleside it is about 2½ miles along the Keswick road. Park in the car park on the common. Walk down to the river Rothay and then walk upstream to the footbridge. Cross it and go directly upwards into the wood. The track is soon well-defined. At the fork keep upwards, and at the end of the wood go through the kissing-gate. Beyond is a track onto open fell. Turn right onto it and climb. This is a very short steep section; the zig-zag way by the wall requires the least effort. The seat near the top offers an excellent view back over Rydal Water. The fell here is in the management of the National Trust and there is free public access. But your walk continues over the brow of the hill. There is a glimpse of the foot of Grasmere Lake, and there is a view over the river to Pennyrock wood, a National Park public access area. The footbridge below connects the National Trust access to the National Park access area. Confused? Not to worry—as far as the public are concerned it means that one can recreate oneself freely on both.

There is a quarry waste heap from an old quarry to the left of the track as you proceed. If the slate is searched, a piece can usually be found with a pattern of ripples. Cut and polished, this type of slate is very decorative. Strike the slates together and they sound almost metallic with hardness. These two qualities have helped to make the Lake District slate highly valued all over the world.

As you walk further round along the track a fuller view of the lake is opened up with a rough-cragged summit of Helm Crag behind. The shape of the 'Lion and the Lamb' is not too obvious from this point.

The best view of the lake is at the seat just before the track is broken away by a beck. Close beyond this beck a faint track can be seen descending to the lake shore. Descend this slowly. A bog near the bottom can be avoided by turning left just before the little

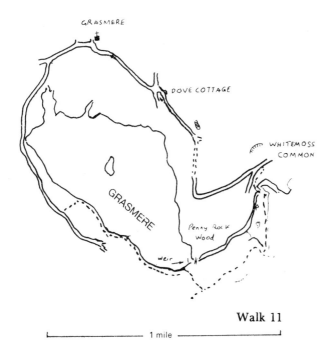

GRASMERE

DOVE COTTAGE

WHITEMOSS
COMMON

GRASMERE

Penny Rock
Wood

Weir

Walk 11

|———————— 1 mile ————————|

hawthorn tree, to follow another small beck down. The lake shore is another place to linger before turning left along it to a wall and a kissing-gate leading into Deerbolts Wood. Turn down to lake shore again and continue on. You soon leave the wood by a stile. There is now a permissive footpath continuing by the lake shore shingle. The fields are farmed and are not open to the general public so you should keep to the path. Delightful views over the lake and its island open up. The fell on the right, at the head of the lake and most dominant, is Seat Sandal (2,365 ft). The path continues over stiles and goes behind a boat-house. Note the 'sculptured' fragment of an old ash tree which still manages to survive. If the views are clear the photographers might use this as 'foreground interest'. At another boat-house the lake-shore path ends and the permissive path turns sharp left to the road above through a stile.

Join the road and turn down right. This should not be a busy road, but watch for traffic and keep well in. Walk right down to the village. At the first junction on the approach, turn right, and go past the nursery to join the T junction. Here, at the first cottage on the left, is a National Trust information centre. Turn right to St Oswald's Church. Enter the churchyard by the second gate. The

Church, the oldest part of which dates back to the 13th century, is worth a visit. Its alterations over the years make it an architectural curiosity, but of course it is famous for its Wordsworth associations. The floor of the church until the 19th century was earthen, and was strewn with rushes. The rush-bearing ceremony is still followed by the local children on the Sunday nearest to St Oswald's day (5th August).

The graveyard is on the eastern side of the church. William Wordsworth and his wife Mary are buried under a simple stone near the river side. Dora Quillinan, their daughter, is buried in the next grave. North of these can be found the grave of Hartley Coleridge, the eldest son of Samual Taylor Coleridge, the great poet who was Wordsworth's friend of earlier days. Hartley, himself a writer, lived at Nab Cottage overlooking Rydal Water.

Leaving the church, cross the bridge, and continue on. The field on the left is the scene of the well-known Grasmere Sports. At the main road junction cross with care and go up the lane directly opposite. Dove Cottage will shortly be seen, standing back a little on the left shortly after the first buildings. It was the home of Wordsworth in his most inspired years between 1799 and 1808. Afterwards, for twenty years, it was the home of Thomas De Quincey, a prolific writer of his day. The house is open to the public on weekdays. A Wordsworth museum is opposite, down the little lane.

Continue up the road until a duck pond is reached. Turn right along the road just after this. As this road is ascended another view of Grasmere opens up on the right. At the top of the road the woodland is left, and the road is on open fell with a view down to Rydal Water. A better view can be obtained from the grass bank to the left, but the lake is in view all the way down to the road to Whitemoss Common, and our starting point.

O.S. 1:50,000 Sheet No. 90

William Wordsworth was a resident of Rydal for 37 years. He must have spent much of his later years just looking at Rydal Water. Now the traffic thunders by the little crag at the eastern end of the lake where he used to sit, and nobody notices it. In fact, if it was not for the close proximity of the A591 all along its northern shore, Rydal Water would be even more of a Mecca than it now is. It is a gem best viewed in the quiet solitude of the breaking dawn.

The walk described must have been done by Wordsworth hundreds of times. It goes along the lake shore, by the old track below Nab Scar, and passes Rydal Mount, his home. The walk starts at White Moss Common. This is about two miles from Ambleside on the Grasmere/Keswick road, the A591. Shortly after passing alongside the shore of Rydal Water, which is on the left, there are reedbeds, then very shortly afterwards the open area of White Moss Common comes into view. The main car park is on the right. Signal early, and take care, as this is a fast road. From Grasmere White Moss Common is reached after one and a half miles. When the shore of Grasmere is left, the road swings sharply through woodlands to the left. Where the wood ends the common begins. Look for the main car park in the old quarry on the left.

On leaving the car walk towards Ambleside, and before reaching the bridge, turn left up the stony track. As this climbs it becomes a green track, and at the top joins a well-defined track at a T junction. There is a little pool to the left of this point. Wordsworth used to skate here, but now it has been taken over by equisetum, a weed sometimes called 'horsetail' or 'devil's fingers'. A walk up the hillside to the left offers some pleasant views.

At this T junction turn right. The track, changing to a footpath, is clear all the way, between walls. After a while there are open fields to the right, then open woodland containing trees which must have been old when Wordsworth walked this way. The track ends at Hart Head, the top of the hamlet of Rydal. Rydal Mount, Wordsworth's home until his death in 1850, is seen below on the right.

Turn right and descend. The entrance to Rydal Mount will be seen, right. (Open to the public.) Descend down the hard road. The entrance to Rydal Hall will then be seen on the left. This was the seat of the Le Flemings, one of the Lake District's largest landowners at one time. Rydal Hall is now a conference centre, and not open to the public.

Continue down, past the church. If the daffodils are in bloom, go

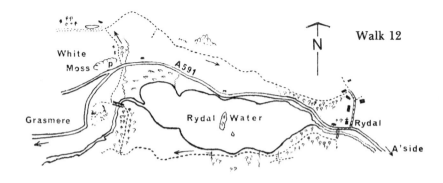

through the churchyard, and into the little wood beyond — Dora's Field. The flowers here were planted for his daughter, Dora, by Wordsworth. The site of the church was also chosen by the bard. He occupied a front pew, but voiced his dissatisfaction at some of the interior detail which was unrectified for a long time. Continue down to the main road. Cross the road with care, turn right. In a short distance, looking left you will see a footbridge. Cross this to the far side into the wood, and turn right. The path wanders through a wood, with the river Rothay coming out of Rydal Water, on the right. It ends at a kissing-gate, and the lake is in front.

Follow the path which goes along the lake shore. This is an accepted public access area, and you can wander about or sit as you please. (The fishing is private.) Continuing on the lake shore path, a wall is reached and you must leave the lake, go through the gateway and follow the track on. After about half a mile there is woodland over the wall on the right, and the path climbs steeply ahead. Look for a kissing-gate through the wall on the right. However, before going through it, if your energy is up to it, a climb to the brow of the hill ahead gives a grand view back across Rydal Water. There is a seat on this high point.

Go through the kissing-gate and descend through the wood. Ignore path right (not a right of way) but continue down. The path at the bottom goes through a wettish section, and soon there is a footbridge. Cross it and you are on the lower portion of White Moss Common. Follow the path round right to the car parks.

O.S. 1:50,000 Sheet No. 90

Two popular walks from Grasmere are to Easedale Tarn and to Allcock Tarn. Both stand at over 1,000 feet above sea level. The walk to the first is not recommended as the usual path, by Sourmilk Ghyll, is very rough and has a record of minor accidents. (Minor, in Mountain Rescue circles, means broken ankles and legs). Easedale, too, is one of the muddiest areas of the central Lake District. Allcock Tarn, on the opposite side of the valley, on the other hand, although a few feet higher, can be reached with care by the ordinary walker not equipped for the high fells, provided that there is no mist and no ice and snow. It is, however, a testing climb and it is not a good idea to attempt it on the first day of a holiday. The not-so-young should take a great deal of time over the ascent. Those with heart conditions (other than romantic) should not attempt it at all. The beauty of the walk is really in the descent.

Park your car in Grasmere village. Broadgate Meadow car park is the best position. It is the first car park one sees on approaching the village centre from Keswick; it is through the village centre, and just on the way out towards Keswick, from the Ambleside side. Leave the car park and turn towards Keswick. Before joining the Ambleside to Keswick road, the road from the village forks. Take the right fork which joins the road opposite the Swan Hotel. Cross the road with care and go up the road to the right of the Swan. Bend left with this road and ignore the junction right. Shortly after this junction a narrow lane will be seen on the right going up between stone walls. At first glance it could be mistaken for a private drive but although it is surfaced it has no gate. The lane goes up alongside a blithe, tumbling beck in a gully pleasantly green with mosses and ferns. There is a gate at the top. Go through this, and immediately turn right over the footbridge. Follow the footpath, which goes up with the ghyll on the left and the wall on the right. The path turns right to follow the wall and an ascent is made of some neat stone steps, put in by someone to ease the way of walkers a long time ago. Path eventually turns left still following the wall but after following it round to a gateway, it leaves the wall and ascends by a grassy path. The stone bridge that you can see below houses the Manchester Corporation pipeline from Thirlmere. After a few minutes, look back. The nearest fell across the valley is Helm Crag. On the craggy summit, on the left, you should make out the shape of the Lion and the Lamb.

The path runs upwards, still between the ghyll left, and the wall out on the right. The ghyll is Greenhead Ghyll, and the valley is the

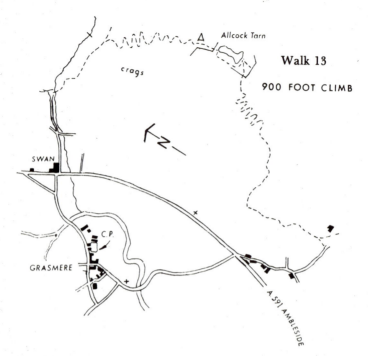

Allcock Tarn

crags

SWAN

C.P.

GRASMERE

A.591 AMBLESIDE

scene of Wordsworth's 'Michael'. The way is steep and you are advised to take the path steadily. When the wall bends off farther to the right, take the branch path to the right to follow the wall direction. This is important. Allcock Tarn is above and to the right. The path that ascends all the way with the ghyll goes on to the Fairfield ridge — over two miles off course and 1,500 feet higher. You presently leave the wall with a slight turn left to ascend stone steps, but still leaving the ghyll at an angle and still climbing. The path then zig-zags, and in places divides as panting walkers have tried variations, but it re-joins further on. The important thing is to keep on climbing. There are occasional rock steps, and the path turns between crags. The path eventually levels out a little. A wall can again be seen in front running parallel with the path, which bears left a little on grass. This point, if you look towards Helm Crag, looks level with that crag's summit. You are in fact only a little lower. To its left you can see up Easedale. The waterfall is Sourmilk Ghyll.

As the path levels, the beck from Allcock Tarn falls to its left. In places where the grass has not covered the path, it can be seen that in fact the path was once paved in places over the softer ground. The wall is again near to the path at the other side of an outcrop, and there is a cairn at the path side. Round the outcrop an iron gate will be seen in a wall ahead and a National Trust sign. Keep to right to

avoid a bog. Go through the iron wicket gate and you are at the tarn.
It is unsafe for non-swimmers.

Continue on the path to the right of the tarn. At the far end just
above the dam there are some fine views. Ahead Windermere can be
seen and, if conditions are clear, right beyond to Morecambe Bay.
The mountains from left to right are the Coniston Old Man range,
with Wetherlam on its right; Pike o'Blisco and the nobbly summits
of Crinkle Crags; Bowfell; The Langdale Pikes; High Raise; Ullscarf.
Nearer and to the right of Helm is Steel Fell. The Helvellyn range is
to the right of this.

The main path continues past the dam to an iron gate but your
path branches right off it to a wall gap with iron bar across it. Climb
over this iron hurdle with care. At the other side bear left a little
round a crag and then bear right, and go between crags. There is an
eagle's-eye view of Grasmere village. A grass track descends towards
the village but there is a branch, left, to a crag viewpoint which is
worth taking. This commands the best view of the village and
Grasmere Lake with its attractive island. From the crag the path goes
off right then zig-zags left, and meanders pleasantly on grass. In
places the path is built up on terraces and there are fine views across
Grasmere. It crosses a small bridge over a waterfall, follows the beck
down, and enters among some weather-beaten larches. Eventually
you reach an iron wicket gate which bears the notice 'Brackenfell'.
The owners of this land allow the public to use this path provided
that no litter is left or damage done to trees, hedges etc. All gates
must be closed. In other words this is a 'permissive footpath'. It is
not a right of way. As an intelligent, responsible and decent person
however, you are allowed to use it. The terraced path eventually
reaches a point near a yew tree. Ignore gate in wall but continue
on our pleasant grassy zig-zags. Looking right from about here over
Dunmail Raise, if conditions are clear, there will be a view of
Skiddaw to the north of Keswick.

The path passes a little fish pond overhung by larch trees, takes a
dive under a spruce tree, presently turns left, and there is a little crag
on the right which gives another good view over Grasmere. You then
go through an iron gate and into a wood and between a fence and a
wall. Go through the wooden gate, into the open and along a hard
track. When this joins the macadam lane by an iron seat, turn right
and descend, to cut the corner, by the narrow path. The lane is
joined to the right of the duck pond. Turn right. At the foot of this
hill, behind the two yew trees on the right is Dove Cottage, the home
of William Wordsworth in his most productive period. Continue to
main road. Cross with care and go down the road opposite into
Grasmere village and the car park.

The slim monument cairn on the summit of Latterbarrow, north-east of Hawkshead, can be seen from many of the viewpoints from Langdale to Kirkstone. It is obviously worth a visit. To make an attractive round walk from Hawkshead the route begins along what years ago was a public road from Hawkshead to a ferrycrossing of Windermere at Belle Grange. It is a woodland walk with views and finishes at the open fell at Latterbarrow. After wet weather bog can be a nuisance in one or two places, but the worst places may be avoided with care.

Park on the village car park. Leave by the car park main entrance, turn right to the T junction, then turn left as if you were going to Windermere via the Ferry. On reaching the first road junction turn left — signposted to Wray Castle and Wray. You are very soon in the hamlet of Colthouse. The Quakers were once strongly in evidence about this area and could not have failed to have had some influence on William Wordsworth's formative years, as he went to school at Hawkshead. There is a seventeenth century Meeting House in Colthouse, with an old burial ground. On approaching the hamlet the slate fence will be noted on the right. There are many of these fences alongside the fields in this area. At first junction continue left, through the hamlet, and continue left again. Shortly after this a lane will be seen leading off to the left. Not many yards beyond this the road widens on the right. From this a private drive before you leads upwards from gates. The track required leads from the gate opposite this, directly on your right, leaving the road at an acute angle.

As you go up this lane a wet patch can be avoided by walking at a higher level left. There is a good view of the Coniston Old Man range on the right as you ascend. There is an attractive combination of larch trees and silver birch on the hillside on the left. After a while a stone wall from the right is approached by a little beck. Go through the gate in the slate fence. There is a mixed wood on the right. The views are really all behind and you should stop occasionally to look back. As the wood finishes on the right, there is an attractive glimpse of Esthwaite Water. Presently a walled woodland is close to the path, on the left, called Renny Crags Wood, and a beck is crossed by a footbridge. Fishpond Wood is very soon approached on the right, and the fishpond can be seen through pine trees. The mud is difficult to avoid here after wet weather. Left hand side is the best. Many larch trees have been planted in this area. Larch wood is commonly used for fence posts, as it is so resinous that it has a high rot-resistance and does not need creosoting. On approaching a gate there is another wet section which can be avoided on the left.

Sitka spruce trees soon predominate left and right. They are the commonest forest tree planted as they are very adaptable to soil conditions and grow very fast. They are distinguishable from the Norway Spruce — the common 'Christmas tree' — by their very prickly needles, which are grey-looking on the underside. As you climb over a brow a sudden view of the High Street range opens up, and there is a view of the Fairfield range to the left. On approaching a gate there is another wet section which can be avoided left.

On the other side of this gate there should be a signpost. If the vandals have not damaged it there should be an arm pointing left for Latterbarrow and one pointing right on for Belle Grange and the ferry. You turn sharp left immediately through this gate, and on the left there is a high deer fence which you must cross by a wooden ladder stile. A footpath follows the fence downwards; take this, keeping the fence to the right. From now onwards, all the way to Latterbarrow, there should be occasional white paint marks, as this is part of the way-marked Claife Heights path which was made by the National Park Planning Board, and largely 'engineered' by National Park wardens. Presently an old wall is seen on the right, and on reaching a gateway in this, the path turns off to the left to climb a short and very steep bank to a wall gap by a silver birch tree. Climb this with care and console yourself with the thought that this is the worst section of the walk. After emerging through the wall, turn right and follow it. A view of Windermere lake opens up with a view of Ambleside. The fells behind are Fairfield and Red Screes, which overlook Kirkstone Pass.

The path turns left before a wall is reached and can be seen fairly well on the ground. The tall cairn on Latterbarrow is now visible and Langdale Pikes well behind are glimpsed to its right, curving towards Latterbarrow. Before reaching a wall turn off to the left to a wall gap. If you have taken your time it has probably taken an hour to reach this point. Just after this gap in the wall there is an apparent fork in the path. The one on the right is a short-cut to Latterbarrow, going through a tricky trap-stile in a deer fence. As this is not a right of way it cannot be recommended. The right of way is to the left of the pine tree, indistinct at first as it passes over drains and wet ground, but more distinct beyond on higher ground as it curves left. This soon comes to a corner of two deer fences, and there is a high ladder stile. Climb over this and take the path on the right which zig-zags through the bracken.

This land is in the care of the National Trust and the public can wander anywhere here. The cairn is soon seen. It is an attractive structure crowning an attractive hill. Behind Hawkshead, which can be seen quite clearly is Grizedale Forest. To the right and beyond is the Coniston Old Man range. Its highest point is to the left —

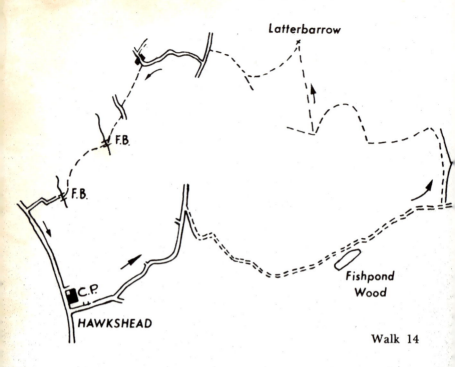

Latterbarrow

F.B.

F.B.

C.P.

HAWKSHEAD

Fishpond
Wood

Walk 14

2,631 feet. The nearer mass on the range to the right is Wetherlam.
To the right of the Coniston Old Man range there is a tight group of
little peaks known as Crinkle Crags. The highest point is 2,816 feet.
Pike o'Blisco is nearer and to the right. To the right of this is the
impressive bulk of distant Bowfell; highest point is on the left —
2,960 feet.

Beyond and to the right of Bowfell can be glimpsed the northern
end of the Scafell Pike range — the highest land in England. This is
Great End, a very popular area for snow and ice climbing in winter.
To the right again is Allen Crags and Glaramara. To the right again
is Langdale Pikes and Pavey Arc, High White Stones and Ullscarf,
Armboth Fell (which overlooks Thirlmere) and before it Helm Crag
above Grasmere; Loughrigg Fell, and behind that through the
Dunmail and Thirlmere gap if visibility allows there is a glimpse of
Skiddaw, almost twenty miles away. Right again is the southern end
of the Helvellyn range — Dollywaggon Pike being the nearest peak —
2,810 feet. Then there is the Fairfield horseshoe, Red Screes, and just
below this to its right is the summit of Kirkstone Pass, with its small
inn, one of the highest in England, Caudale Moor and the long
north-aligned ridge of High Street follow. The old track of Garburn

48

Bridge House, Ambleside

Rydal Mount

Hawkshead

Tarn Hows

Pass is at its nearest end, and behind are the fells at the head of Kentmere. To the east are the Pennines and the Yorkshire Dales. Right again, now looking southwards, there are glimpses of Morecambe Bay.

For the best view of Windermere it is necessary to walk a few yards from the summit cairn, easterly. (That is the opposite side to Hawkshead.) The head of the lake makes an attractive picture. Wray Castle is below. To the right of Ambleside is Wansfell, and the wooded slopes of Skelghyll. To the right on the lake shore is Low Wood Hotel. To the right of the picture, on the right of a wood and a group of buildings is Brockhole, the National Park Centre.

Wander any way down towards Hawkshead as all the little paths link up at the bottom. It is as well not to take direct line as this leads to a very steep descent into a hollow. A short diversion to the right is better. Eventually near the bottom a path will be met descending right. This goes through alder trees — a tree of wet places. Although this is a hardwood, on inspection you will see that its seeds are borne in cones. The bog can be avoided in part by going round to the right on higher ground. On the other side of the beck the path is on harder ground. You pass through a gate, and descend through a field to another gate at the road side.

Turn left along the road. A short way along this road take the right turning at the junction to walk along a narrow surfaced road by hedges and slate fences. On reaching a farm — High Loanthwaite Farm — turn left through the little concrete yard and go through the gate. It could be muddy here for a short section. Go forward across the fields by the footpath. It descends with a hedge on the left and through a gate by an ash tree. It continues to descend, rather less distinct, alongside a fence, to a wicket gate by an oak tree. Through this gate join the lane and turn left, and after fifty yards turn right through the slate stile. Go across the field, bearing slightly left, towards the bottom of a wall where another slate stile will be seen. Go forward across the field, keeping the boggy area nearby, to the right. Very shortly go through the slate stile by the side of a small section of wall on the right. Cross the drain in the next field by a bridge. Bear slightly left to cross field. Make it a wide curve left to follow the higher land if the field is boggy, then right. Make for a slate stile to the left of a group of trees. It is approached by a short slate bridge over a drain. Go forward towards Hawkshead village to a fence and bear left to follow it. At the end of it go through the gate onto the footbridge, and follow the path onto the village centre. Left for car park past the National Trust Information Centre and the post office.

This is largely a walk across fields. After wet weather fields can be very muddy. There is also a ford to cross. Ergo — this is a walk for well-fitting Wellington boots in all but very dry weather, unless you can tolerate wet feet. You may note that the text for this walk is long. It is just that the route across the fields is so difficult to see that more explanation is needed. If you like solitude this has an advantage; for the only people you are likely to meet on this walk are (a) local villagers who know their way around; (b) exceptional map readers with exceptional maps; (c) folk like yourself with copies of this book clutched in their hands.

Wray Castle is about the half-way mark and is a good place for your picnic. The building is bogus — a Victorian folly occupied by a school, but the grounds down to Lake Windermere are open to the public as the whole property is owned by the National Trust. There are some fine trees in the grounds, and there is one with a label stating it was planted by William Wordsworth himself. So you can make this walk last as long as you like.

Park in the public car park in the village of Hawkshead. Walk down the narrow main street until, just after the National Trust Information Centre, you come to the gable end of the Red Lion. Go down the alley right and see the type of 'yard' community-living that typifies old Lake District villages. The habit of building thus sprang from the need to guard against raids from the Scots. (The alley entrances were gated.)

Cross the by-pass road and continue on by a high wall along a track and path to a foot-bridge. Turn left after the bridge to follow the bank of the stream for a short distance, then incline right to a wicket gate in a corner between a hedge and a fence. It will probably be muddy. Cross a slate bridge, then walk across the field, very slightly right, to a slate stile via a bridge over a ditch. Turn left and to another stile and straight ahead for another onto a lane. Turn left.

After fifty yards or so, go through the wicket gate on right alongside the oak tree. Follow the fence, through a gate then to a better defined track towards the farm. Go right of the buildings and yard and go through the gate onto a lane. Turn left. Just after the farmhouse on right go through gate, and along a lane. Gate and stile. Do not bend left with the track but continue on by a line of trees to gate-posts. Go on, on the same line, to stile, deviating slightly at the end to cross the ditch by the fence. In the next field bear left and make for the higher part of field. A corner can then be seen ahead where two lines of trees (once hedges) meet. Make for this. Blelham

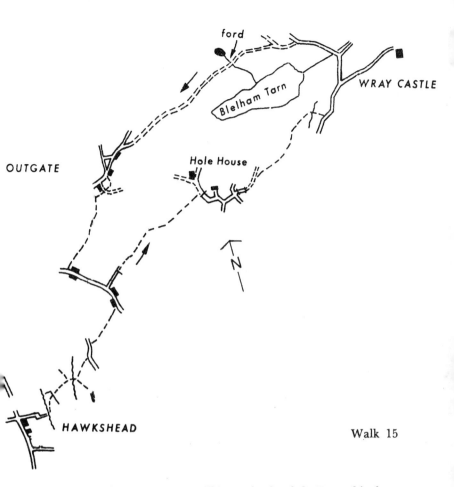

ford

Blelham Tarn

WRAY CASTLE

OUTGATE

Hole House

N

HAWKSHEAD

Walk 15

Tarn can now be seen. A barn will be noticed to left. From this there is a wall upwards. Ignore the first gate in it and make for the gate in the corner to the right of it, slightly hidden by a knoll. Through this gate there is an old lane right; its wetness can be avoided by taking to the ridge to its left — all that remains of the hedge. Over stile and right to macadam road.

Turn left through the farmyard and through the gate beyond. There is a good track past an unusually gnarled ash tree. You will have to be content with just looking at Blelham Tarn as there is no public access to it. Duck spotters will need binoculars. The area is a National Nature Reserve under the control of the Nature Conservancy, as it is an almost unique example of Sphagnum bog developing from wet willow woodland. The Freshwater Biology

51

Association also take an active interest in it, and if there are buoys in the tarn it will be one of their experiments. Continue straight on to the small wood. Here the way seems barred; be not dismayed, there is a slate stile left. Through the stile the hedge should be followed to another stile, and further with hedge towards a wooded knoll. Skirt it to the left, then go through the trees to a kissing-gate and slate bridge. Go ahead, following the hedge on the right. Go through gate into macadam road, and turn left. Cut the corner by following the fence on the left, and soon there is the stone gateway to Wray Castle on the right.

Leaving Wray Castle by the same gateway, turn right and follow road round and over the bridge until, just short of a single large beech tree, there is a gate, left. Go through this, take track beyond and at its junction just inside bear left, and on to gate where track leads into silver birches. There is now a wet section and it will not surprise you to learn that you are near to the sphagnum bog which so interests the scientists. This is a pleasant wood and you are soon at a ford. (If the water is deep, gentlemen may here carry the ladies.)

Go through gate and notice the hundreds of old ant hills. At head of tarn path does not turn left as it would appear, but follows wall to right and through a gate to a green track. There are good views to tarn and beyond to fells, as the path rises. There is another gate and the path passes between fir plantations, and eventually a gate leads out onto the Ambleside-Hawkshead road at Outgate (or in local parlance 'Ootyat'). Turn left. At the far gable end of Outgate Inn turn left and go through the gate immediately afterwards, and a kissing-gate immediately after that. Bear right to corner and climb over stile, and then across lane to climb the next stile. Go across the field towards gate but do not go through—there is a stile fifty yards to its right, leading into woodland. A meandering path among the trees crosses a small beck, goes round holly trees and left by slate gate post, then right to the gate at right of the farm buildings. A second gate leads onto a macadam lane. Turn left. If you can look at the front of the farmhouse here without embarrassing the inhabitants, it is a typical example of a fine old Lake District dwelling. Further on you should recognise the next farm—it is Loanthwaite again and we go through the gate after the farm buildings and along the path to the village by the route on which the walk started.

This is a forest walk. To anyone interested in natural history forests are a delight. When the land is broken and craggy even the mono-culture indulged in by the Forestry Commission offers interest. At the moment the Commission do not make the visitors unwelcome as they once did. However they are not yet geared to accepting walkers. Their bulldozers tear through the rights of way. Footpaths are made into forest roads, and new branches lead off in all directions. Maps are soon outdated. Even their own maps, on sale to the public at their information centre at Grizedale, are not up to date. Furthermore you need to be an expert to sort out the tangle of trails. Some paths are mercifully colour-marked. Follow the route detailed here carefully, however, and all should be well.

During mid-summer months anti-fly cream might be needed, particularly if the weather is 'muggy'. Most of the wet patches are avoidable with care. The walk begins at Hawkshead. Park the car at Hawkshead Car Park. Leave the car park at the entrance to the village, and cross the road towards the church. Go through the iron gate. The Grammar School, where William Wordsworth was educated, is on the right. Go through the iron wicket gate into the churchyard. At path junction in the churchyard turn left. Leave by the iron wicket gate, and continue on footpath with the slate fence on the right. Go through wooden wicket gate and at Y junction turn right. This path shortly turns right through another wooden wicket gate, follows a wall, then goes through an iron kissing-gate. Go along path between wall and slate fence to an access road. Continue on to a T junction, turn left. Pass through an old stone gateway and up past the buildings. Track then changes to a footpath and goes upwards between fences in open woodland. The path is joined by a beck, and it is hard to decide which is path and which beck. It then bears left and climbs upwards through blackthorn scrub. Path comes to wooden gate which is the boundary of Grizedale Forest.

Curve left and continue climbing parallel with fence on the left. Cross the beck, left, and continue climbing with fence. Beech have been planted alongside the wood. Farther on the beeches can be seen to have been damaged by browsing deer, and probably sheep too. At the forest road turn left. Quite shortly after this a ride will be seen on the right of the road, following an old broken wall. This is the right of way. Turn right and follow the footpath. A forest road crosses the path eventually, and there is a forest road opposite. This is the right of way. It leads into a wild life sanctuary area which should be treated with respect. Keep quiet on this section of the walk. Keep

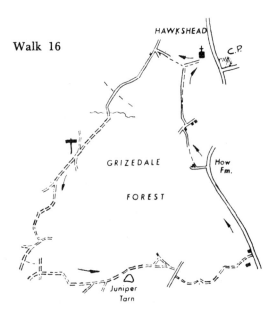

Walk 16

HAWKSHEAD

C.P.

GRIZEDALE

How Fm.

FOREST

Juniper
Tarn

dogs on lead. Do not wander the slightest bit off the path, and all should be well.

As previously stated the walk goes across and onto the forest road opposite. At the road junction continue left. The road falls and comes to a T junction. Turn right. And at the junction very shortly afterwards, bear left, and down the hill. Very shortly again, a beck comes down from the right and goes under the road through a culvert. Just after this there is a ride on the left. It should have a yellow and red marker on it and this is the way to go. From now on the yellow and red markers mark your way. You could assume that you are out of the wild life sanctuary area.

Go down the ride which becomes a road. Not very far along this road, at a point just before the road widens out where there is a loading bay for timber, there is a yellow and red marked path down to the left through the trees alongside a beck. It starts down the steep bank. Go down with care and follow it. Follow the path down with the beck, and when the forest closes in left, cross the beck. This leads on to a forest road, turn left. The road is joined by others from the right, but continue straight on. After this there is a fox-proof fence and a tarn where wildfowl are raised. This is Juniper Tarn.

The road is joined by one from the left. Continue on. There is another road in from the left and, continuing on, you come to a cattle-grid and the way out of the forest. At the public road turn right. After sixty yards turn left through wicket gate. This track could now have white markers on it. Continue on down this track to the farm buildings of High Barn. Go through gate and down to a wooden gate at the end of the buildings. Continue on this line, and follow the ridge of an old hedge line bearing left. Soon on the left is a hollow. To avoid the wetness near the gate ahead, it is recommended that this hollow be circled, and at the far end the fence and wall followed down to the gate. Go through gateway and continue on the same line, wall on right. Drop down to track on the right. Go along on a ridge between two becks. After crossing the right-hand stream, which is culverted under the path, the path curves right and then left, and descends to a corner where it is crossed by a beck. Go on then through the gate and along a good track through woodland. The beck is in a ravine below. The track crosses the beck at the bottom and goes through a farmyard. Go between the buildings, join the public road, and turn left.

Even a minor road such as this one can be unpleasant for walkers, and a public footpath which follows the road direction at higher level on the left is recommended. Watch for the lane on the left which should be signposted. This is How Farm. Turn left. Just before the gable end of the building on the right, turn right. Go through a gate and, at the end of the building, turn left through another gate and, then right to follow the wall. There is an iron wicket gate at the end. Cross the slate bridge and turn left up the driveway. Continue along access road through buildings. Join the public road and turn right. Shortly after this watch for public footpath between walls on the left. This is a pleasant hard-surfaced footpath. After two kissing-gates and a wooden gate, the tower of Hawkshead church can be seen ahead. Go through wooden gate, and then the iron gate of the churchyard. Turn right at the path junction and go past the Grammar School again.

Tarn Hows is the name of a farmhouse in the wooden heights above Monk Coniston. It is now, however, the popular name of the nearby lovely tarn. Every visitor to the Lake District should go there for it is considered one of the finest beauty spots in the country. The tarn is one of the most photographed pieces of water in Britain, and large murals of its likeness (sometimes with exotic flowers superimposed in the foreground) are frequently seen in hotels, public halls and private homes. The fact that it is water raised to an artificial level, and planted about by largely alien trees, makes no difference. The effect, particularly in the early morning or the evening, is moving.

Its advantages are that it can be reached all the way by car; (though this can be a disadvantage in a bank-holiday crush) and that the whole area is open to the public as it is owned by the National Trust. Most motorists are content to look, then drive away. Some set off to walk around the tarn, about two miles, but are often deterred by the wet paths at the far end. By comparison, few know about the exciting views from the heathery crags on its western hill — Tom Heights. At its northern crag one has the impression of standing on a dais in a colossal amphitheatre. The great walls and buttresses of the fells are all around; and if anything is lacking to stir you it could only need the addition of an ancient pagan altar and perhaps some great Wagnerian music.

It is a walk for a clear day. Time should be allowed for negotiating awkward ground around rock outcrops and boggy earth. Drive on past the view of the tarn to the main car park at the end. Walk out of the entrance and descend by the track opposite to the left-hand corner of the tarn. Go through the gateway and along the short dam. After leaving the dam ascend to the left front by a footpath, through the trees. (Tom Heights is covered in paths, mainly sheep tracks, and this suggested route will be joined by these at times.) The route leads upwards through small rock outcrops to a small crag. From here the nearer fell in view is Holme Fell. Coniston Old Man is the large fell left, Wetherlam being the great nearer arm. The summit cairn 'The Old Man' itself can be seen towards the left. ('Man' is a local name for a high cairn.) Langdale Pikes are to the right. Go forward towards the right on a footpath. It passes a mountain ash tree then goes to the left of a holly tree. Shortly after this bear right between rock outcrops, gaining height. The next crag is higher, and from it can be seen a good stretch of Coniston lake. Towards the

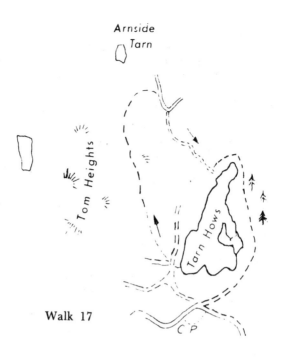

Arnside Tarn

Tom Heights

Tarn Hows

Walk 17

C P

Langdales, and left of the Pikes, can be seen Bowfell; nearer is Pike o'Blisco, then Crinkle Crags.

Make your way through the heather to the next crag, which is a little to the right and should bear a summit cairn. This crag is higher than the last and the views open up further. To the right is a glimpse of Windermere. Move forward through the heather to the next summit, which should also bear a cairn. This shows up the northern fells. The summit of Helvellyn can be seen in clear weather; Dollywaggon is its nearest peak. The gap to right of this is Grisedale. There are a number of Grisedales or Grizedales in the Lake District. This one is the high pass over which King Dunmail is said to have fled after his defeat by King Edmund on Dunmail Raise in 945. To the right is the Fairfield range, and High Street. The Pennines can be seen far to the right. Go forward again along the summit ridge to the next high point. This is the most northerly point also crowned by a cairn. Add your rock contribution to it, then admire what you see. If this drama fails to stir your soul to some degree, little else may in this world — and there is probably little hope for you in the next!

The tarn glimpsed ahead is not part of Tarn Hows, but is Arnside Tarn. If you walk to the left-hand edge of the ridge for a few yards, you can look down on another tarn alongside the Ambleside-Coniston road — Yewtree Tarn. Standing at the cairn facing north, that is the way you faced at the arrival, Tarn Hows is to the right and back. There are quite a few paths back. Some are steep and some are boggy. The recommended way is to go forward, curving right in a semi-circle on less testing ground. Descend to a small hollow and pick up a faint path going left, through grass. Continue in this direction through the bracken and heather, until you are confronted by a small heather-covered crag. Turn right on path here, descending through the bracken. On reaching a damp hollow, follow path turning right again. The spruce and larch trees of the plantation of Tarn Hows should now be seen. The path meanders towards these woods losing height, towards their corner. A wet track is joined which comes from the right. Turn left along it. (At this point it might be as well to warn the uninitiated on how to tell wet ground from dry without standing in it. Wet ground grows rushes, or fat lush-looking green grass. Bracken or heather will not tolerate very wet land.) Follow the path, avoiding the wetness by taking to the higher edge, and this curves right to a wooden step-stile. This is a clearer path leading to another step-stile. Go through the trees to the T junction with another track. Turn left. This comes to the edge of the Tarn. Cross the beck by a wooden bridge.

This is the track which circles the tarn. You cross another bridge, another stile, then four more bridges, avoiding mud and bog as best you can. There are several ways from this end of the tarn. You could follow the tarn edge. But the recommended route is to take the distinct track which seems to leave the tarn after the bridges, following a fence on the left by handsome pine trees. This track bears right at a point in the fence where there is a gate, and goes under larches and pines. At the track fork, take the right hand one which goes closer to, and overlooks, the tarn. Some of the best views of the tarn are from this track.

There is a stile at the end of the track. Beyond this the track joins the macadam road back to the car park right. However, a short cut over a pine-clad promontory is more pleasant.

This is a very varied walk, through woodland which is almost jungle in places; out onto high vantage points; and alongside the quiet waters of two lovely tarns. You should take at least three hours on this walk, not counting a meal time, to allow for breathers, and to admire the views, and to dawdle. There is the chance of seeing wild deer; both the red deer, Britain's largest mammal, and the roe (the small dainty deer) the country's most beautiful animal. Both are more easily seen in winter, but there is a chance at any time. The signs of both—the tracks in soft ground, and the stripping of bark on young trees—are certain to be seen by those who are observant.

The walk starts at Far Sawrey. This is the first hamlet one comes to after crossing the ferry from Windermere *en route* to Hawkshead; and from Hawkshead towards the ferry it is the second hamlet; Near Sawrey coming first (being nearer to Hawkshead) and Far Sawrey shortly afterwards. Find somewhere to park in Far Sawrey without obstructing entrances or gates. A telephone box will be seen by the Sawrey Hotel, and alongside it is a lane leading up-hill beyond and above the hotel. Go up this, go through the gate, and just beyond it take the fork right. Look left for a view of the Sawreys. This is 'Peter Rabbit' country—for Beatrix Potter, creator of this great character of literature, with Tom Kitten, Jemima Puddleduck and others—lived at Near Sawrey.

Near the top of the hill note the 'hog-hole' in the stone wall on the left, to allow sheep access to both sides while retaining the cattle. At the top of the hill go through the gate, and then take the lane between the walls on the left. Unless the vandals have got there first there should be a signpost here directing us towards Hawkshead. From this point onwards too there should also be white paint markers, as this is part of the Claife Heights route created by the National Park Planning board.

Shortly afterwards the track opens up and wall is on right and a pond or wet area is passed. The path goes between walls again, through a gate, then opens up. There is a plantation left. Presently, the wall begins again on the right and then comes the ruin of a stone barn. Branch right immediately afterwards on a less distinct track and follow the wall.

The path again presently passes between double walls, the left hand one tumbledown, and a stile is reached, below a shattered tree-clothed crag. Go over the stile, and the path will be seen going left, zig-zagging up the hill. This is short and steep. Palpitaters should take it very slowly. Near the top, watch for the sign-post. The route

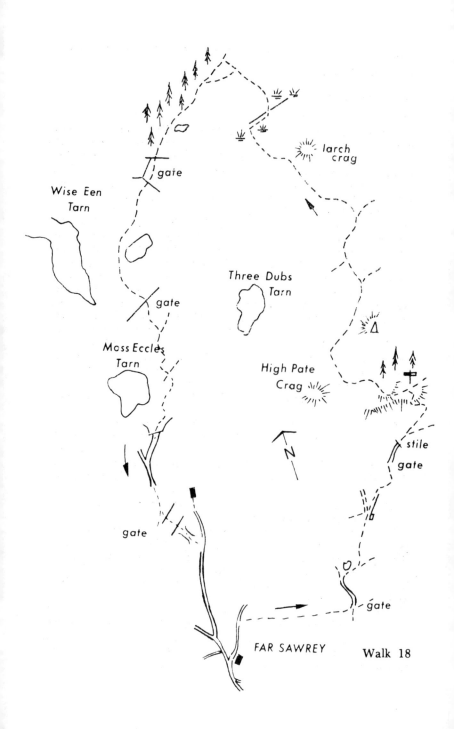

Wise Een
Tarn

gate

gate

Moss Eccles
Tarn

gate

larch
crag

Three Dubs
Tarn

△

High Pate
Crag

N

stile
gate

gate

FAR SAWREY   Walk 18

from this post goes left, and there should be white markers; but go right first, if you wish, to a fair view-point. NB. If path begins to go downhill you have passed the junction by a long way!

Having turned left at this junction you pass over rocky ground. The young trees are sitka spruce — the commonest forest tree. This tree is a native of the western seaboard of North America. (Sitka is a port in Alaska.) It grows very successfully and rapidly in Britain, and is tolerant of wet conditions.

After a while the path rises under what could best be described as a tunnel of sitkas. Then the path is open on the left as crags are met before it turns right immediately afterwards to ascend a crag. This is Low Pate Crag. Here is an airy place to rest. There are views across Windermere to the east, soft rounded slopes of the southern Furness, and to the west the Furness and the Cumbrian fells.

The way off the crag goes directly down another green tunnel to a second view point; High Pate Crag, more set about by trees.

The path from these crags plunges right and down by rocky steps, through a short tree tunnel, crosses a drain, and climbs through another tunnel bearing right, and meanders. Before it again goes downwards there is a crag to the right worth investigating. On it stands a triangulation point erected by Ordnance Survey. This is High Blind How. Go down through another tree tunnel until an apparent T junction is reached. Turn left and along a wider forest ridge. Afterwards a forest road is joined at a T junction. Turn right, along it, for only a short distance. (Note the artificial tarn on left.) After about ninety yards the path leaves the road on the left (watch for waymarks) and goes upwards through the larch trees, changing again to sitkas near the top. The path again opens and falls to cross a drain, then, baring slightly left, ascends through another short tree tunnel on rock steps before opening up onto another small larch-clad crag.

The path then bears left, then right through a wet section with a tumble-down wall on the left. The path afterwards goes left to descend onto a forest road. Cross this road, going left with the waymarks, to a path which meanders left through the trees, parallel with a wet moss on its right. The path then joins a hard forest road at an elbow. Strictly speaking from this point one should go 120 yards to the right to join the right of way, then turn left. However the forest road, left, cuts the corner, and the officers of the Forestry Commission are not likely to shoot you for a mild trespass of a few yards.

The white-marked trail has now been abandoned and the track is now an old bridle-way through a more mature forest. It soon bends left and there is a pool on the left. Beyond it a 'hide' can be seen in a Scots Pine. This could well be occupied by naturalists and should not be approached as you could scare away birds or animals being watched. Permission to use these hides has to be obtained from the Forestry Commission office at Grizedale. The trail now could well be very muddy as it is often used by horses and tractors, but the mud can be avoided by taking it to the right.

Leave the forest at last through a gate and follow the wall down. On the left is a fish pond used by the Freshwater Biology Association for experiments. Keep close to the dam if you wish to avoid wetness. On the right is Wise Een Tarn. The path now becomes more obvious and passes through a gate which should be closed. Other tracks join from the left but continue down and Moss Eccles Tarn is then reached. A place to rest.

The track is then joined by a wall left, passes through a gate and between walls; then, as track falls, the walls widen out as a track joins from the right. The track continues its descent between walls and, before the walls close in again, another wide area is reached. Further down, a Y-junction is reached. The left-hand track goes through a gate. This is the way, and to check its position correctly there should be a house clearly seen across the field to the left. (The first house seen for several miles.) The track is a green one and is well defined. It goes down through a gate and is joined by a beck from the left which it presently crosses by a plank bridge. A macadam track, Cuckoo Brow Lane, is joined. This passes by several buildings to join a public road by the vicarage, and eventually the main Hawkshead-ferry road. The starting point at Sawrey Hotel is to the left.

Claife Heights is the fell facing you across the lake from Windermere. It is densely wooded with mixed woods facing the lake, and above and beyond are the thick plantings of the Forestry Commission. Crier of Claife is on the summit track. Strange title? The crier was a fearsome ghost who haunted these woods. Long ago the first encounter was with the local ferryman, who was with friends in the local hostelry when a cry was heard calling for the ferry. He went out. Later his friends became anxious when he failed to return. They found him wandering. He had been terrified out of his wits. Time and time again afterwards the dreadful cry was heard. The ferryman never recovered. At last the ghost was laid by a priest with bell, book and candle. He banished the horror to a little quarry on the heights of Claife. The spot is marked on Ordnance Survey maps 'Crier of Claife'. So far as is known the cry is not heard in daylight, so you need not worry too much about this! Those who want to take no chances should carry a sprig of rowan (mountain ash). The walk is a pleasant woodland excursion, returning along the shore of Windermere, and is highly recommended. The worst part of the walk is directly at the beginning when it goes steeply for a section. It is always best to get the climbing over with right away. Anyone can do the walk, however. Older folk can climb just as well as young folk. It just takes them a little longer. The walk is wet in parts.

The walk starts at Station Wood which is on the Hawkshead side of the Windermere ferry. From Windermere the car can be parked at one of the Bowness car parks. Follow the footpath which starts at the end of the promenade past the boatyards. This goes by Cockshot Point, along the lake shore, then joins the road down to the ferry. Cross by the ferry. Walk towards Hawkshead, and just past the first road junction a little way along, there is a footpath through a wall gap into a wood. Follow this clear track until you come to a ruined building. From Hawkshead, take the ferry road to Windermere. At the bottom of the steep hill leading to the lake, the road nears the lake shore, and immediately on the left is a car park in a wood. Park here. Walk out by the footpath towards the ferry, then branch left and climb at the sign post. Follow the short but very steep path, waymarked white, to the ruin.

The ruin is the 'station'. This is not to be confused with the transport type of building of this name. A station, in the Lake District's romantic era, was where the discerning visitor was expected to stand, or station himself, to view the classic views. This station belonged to the Ferry Hotel, now no more an hotel. Windows faced

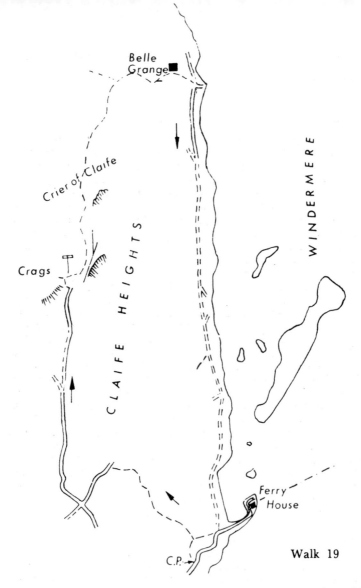

Walk 19

classic views, and were glazed with coloured glass to give added effect.

The path leads upwards from the station and is way-marked with white spots of paint, as this is the path made and marked by the National Park to take in the heights. The path goes between crag faces. The path falls a few steps to a wet area, then climbs through the trees. The climb is steep. The path wanders a little, and near the head of a gully goes off right on a gentle slope, then turns left quite clearly, and zig-zags up to a fence. Turn right and follow fence under mountain ash clump. Go through gap in wall, and path turns left and follows fence. There is a view of the lake and Belle Isle. Bowness Bay with its boat yards is to the right. The path falls and rises, and goes between a fence and a wall, through a wall gap, then between fences between two plantations. On the left there is Japanese Larch, on the right is European Larch. The trees are very similar but there are colour differences in the twigs, and the needles. The Japanese is now more commonly grown as it grows faster. This path ends at a kissing gate and T junction. Turn left. Go through the gate and the track then goes between a fence and a wall. Just after this watch for a gateway on the right to a track going up between two walls. This is the track you want, and it should be way-marked white.

After a while a pool, or a wet patch, is on the left. You go through a gateway. After another interval there is a ruined barn on the right, and just after this the track forks. Take the right-hand fork which follows the wall. Follow this track right through until it reaches a hurdle stile. Go over. The path beyond can be seen climbing steeply left, but this is a short section. Follow it through, ignoring faint turning off to the right. The path zig-zags near the top. Small sitka spruces near the top have been damaged by deer. They have been browsed, and 'frayed' by the deer's antlers. This is the way the roe-bucks mark their territory. There are two wet sections in the path.

Near the summit of this path there should be a signpost on the left. The white waymarks should go off to the left. You turn right however, leaving the waymarks, and onto a good view-point. The right-of-way is over to your left but it is very wet going and you are advised to cross the broken fence and wall at the view-point and pick up a path going left—meandering, but going roughly parallel with the old wall and forest-edge. You can take in some pretty views over Windermere. A beck is crossed at a tricky bit by the wall and the path continues on steeply to a very good look-out point. From here, the path descends to re-join the more clearly-defined right-of-way where it has left the conifer forest to enter the broad-leafed wood. The path meanders through the bracken. Wet sections can be avoided left or right. Presently the path shows better preservation, the lower side of it being built up. Here there are good views across the lake. The two small islands towards the far shore are Lady Holme and, the smaller one, St Mary's Chapel. There was once a resident monk here, but the chapel is now a ruin. The path enters mixed woodland again, and you are now in the area of the Crier of Claife. The pylon on the left above is a radio relay station.

The path goes along the right of a spruce plantation, then it begins to lose height. It crosses a beck, continues, and joins a track at a T junction. Turn right and go down this track, once well kept but now in ruin. Some of the old paving and cobbling can be seen lower down. The track finishes at the garden wall of Belle Grange. Follow it right to T junction. Turn right to walk along the lake shore. The track goes through the wood, largely Norway Spruce on the right and Douglas Fir on the left, with larch. Pass through the old gateposts. After this you should see some very tall straight Douglas Firs. There are one or two large beech trees on the right. All this land belongs to the National Trust and there is free access.

When the walls of a property ahead are seen (Strawberry Gardens), there is a very fine large sweet chestnut tree on the right. The track passes above Strawberry Gardens and approaches the lake shore again. These woods were once great charcoal producers. The charcoal was made by the very controlled burning of wood. The fire was almost smothered by sods and earth, air being let in very carefully. Earth platforms called 'pitsteads' were dug out by the charcoal burners for their fires. One can be seen up the bank to the right just beyond the Strawberry Gardens boundary. There is now a birch tree growing in the middle of it. There are many pitsteads in this area, now largely lost in the new woods.

There are one or two old beeches along the track side, and views across the lake. Watch for a second old sweet chestnut on the right. The nuts only ripen successfully very occasionally, as they are natives of Spain. They were supposed to have been first introduced into Britain by the Romans. Pass through another old pair of gateposts, and go by the cattle grid. The track becomes a surfaced road.

The island on the left between the shore and the large island of Belle Isle is Thompson Holme (locally 'Tommy Holme'). On the left farther on, a Norway Spruce stands beside a Douglas Fir. These are probably labelled as a National Trust nature trail passes this point. Two islands are now seen on the left between you and Belle Isle. These are the Lilies of the Valley islands; so called because the plant grows wild there. The much overgrown island just before the ferry is Crow Holme. The tiny one before it is Maiden Holme. Go by the cattle grid. You are soon at the T junction with the Hawkshead-Ferry road, which was your starting point. The station is above on the right. Walkers bound for the car park can go through the wall gap which comes after the footpath gap, and walk parallel to the road, in the wood, by some good viewpoints.

Walk 20   Windermere Shore Footpath, South to Lakeside

7½ miles [12 km]

O.S. 1:50,000 Sheet No. 97

A frequent complaint about Windermere is that so little of the shore is accessible to the general public. What is really meant is that the public roads hardly touch upon the shores and it is assumed that there is no way to the lake. As far as the western shore is concerned this is not the case. One can walk from the ferry landing either north or south. Both expeditions are worth while. They are excellent walks on quiet days and are extra-enjoyable in winter when walkers can be rewarded by the sight of many visiting ducks, geese, waders and divers. But the walks should be on the priority list for any time of year.

The walk south from the ferry is marred in parts where it touches upon sections of public roads where there could be traffic hazards even though the roads are minor ones. Sundays in the season can bring this difficulty, with the added one of speed-boat noise. The walk can be wet in sections, as one can expect of a route very close to the shore and low-lying. In flood conditions it could be impassable.

A circular route would be a marathon, so it is suggested that the return journey to the starting point should be made by steamer. The steamer service normally runs from May to September, and it is recommended that a timetable leaflet be collected before the expedition. If the walk is done in an out-of-season period it can finish at Newby Bridge where you can pick up a 'bus. But here again time-tables should be consulted first. Alternatively, but less satisfactorily, the walk could be split into two.

Park in one of the Bowness car parks. From Bowness Pier follow the promenade round past the boathouses and the car park. At the end of the promenade the pavement curves left but a public path turns off right between a hedge and fence. This leads onto Cockshot Point (National Trust). Follow the path round. At first sight here the lake looks very narrow but in fact there is a large island in mid-lake, Belle Isle. The path eventually brings us past the police and lake warden's boat house, and onto a road. Turn right. This leads to Windermere Ferry. Embark. Disembark on the far shore and walk up the road. The large house on the left is Ferry House, and head-quarters of the Freshwater Biology Association. Pass the buildings, and after passing the right-hand side road just round the corner, avoid the road with its blind bend, by going through a wall gap on the right into the wood. Ash Landing Wood, (National Trust.) Follow the road side, climbing through the silver birches, to the top of the small crag. Here there is a lovely view down the lake. The odd-

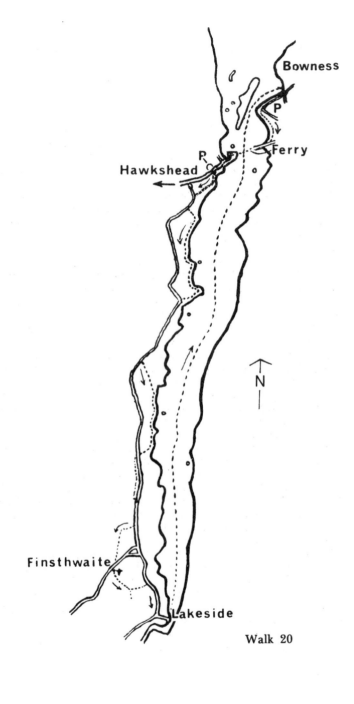

Bowness

P

Ferry

Hawkshead

P

N

Finsthwaite

Lakeside

Walk 20

looking structure on the jetty end on the left of the downward view is Storrs Temple, a folly built in 1804.

Continue on across the informal car park then across the road. Quit the road almost immediately by going along the lane left. The wooded fringe of the lake is on the left, a nursery on the right. The trees thin out to allow lake access, then the lane bends right to avoid properties, and we join a surfaced road. Turn left and walk with care. Presently the wood thins out on the left and there is a stile onto a lake-side field (signposted). Follow the path to the shore, and walk again by the edge of the lake. After crossing a footbridge and a stile, after 120 yards there is a fenced area. Do not be put off by this —the right of way is through the gap and close to the lake shore. Pass the concrete jetties, but before going over the stile look back up the lake and there is a good view of the mountains beyond to the north-east—Yoke, the hump of Ill Bell, then Froswick and Thornthwaite Crag (2,569 feet) on the High Street range.

The path follows a wooded promontory. Just off shore is an attractive little wooded island—Ling Holme. There is next a damp section through reeds, then there is another 'nab' or promontory—Rawlinson Nab. The view up-lake is cut short by Belle Isle. The prominent fell feature in this direction is Red Screes (2,547 feet) above Kirkstone Pass. Down-lake on the other hand the prospect is softer and quite beautiful. Following the track on, there is a reedy island left—Grass Holme—the haunt of swans. Then the path turns off the road, and you are faced with a twenty to thirty minute walk on it after turning left.

If the road is not too busy the walk is enjoyable. There are conifer woods left and hardwoods right, but there is no grass verge offering security against traffic until you being to ascend a hill. Ignore the road's hairpins and take to the path up the grass to the left. At the top of the hill the road levels before a descent. Watch for the gap in the fence, left, which should be signposted. This is an area which was reputed in old times to be haunted by a fearful ghost, but it will not trouble us. Go through the gap and down between the fences. The path steepens under yew trees then turns right, goes behind some property, and eventually reaches the lake again. There is another attractive little island—Silver Holme—before you. Local tradition has it that there is a hoard of silver hidden under the water at this point. A small 'nab' after it gives excellent views up and down the lake. The shore becomes a rock slab known as Long Tongue, and there are more good views. A little further on, the lake must be left again for ahead is private property, in the ownership of the YMCA.

The path leaves the lake shore between a high deer fence on the right and a barbed wire fence, left, and one might get a fleeting impression that this was a concentration camp. The road is then reached. Although only a secondary road it can be busy, and is liable to be dangerous as the highway authority 'robbed' the pedestrian of the grass verge in the course of road widening. Turn left. Go carefully and after a few minutes watch for a gap in the wall into the wood right. Follow the roadside in the wood. This is a very mild trespass on YMCA property in the interests of safety.

After about ten minutes one is again forced onto the road by swamp and steep ground opposite the entrance to the YMCA South Camp. Less than fifteen minutes later you should be at a group of buildings—Stock Park. You must now look at your watch and make a decision. The Lakeside Pier for the steamer is twenty minutes—allow thirty—along the road, which needs even more care after you have turned left at the first junction as there are blind bends. If you have an hour left before steamer time a comfortable and pleasant diversion can be made across the fields to avoid the road hazards.

The detour starts directly after the buildings along a lane on the right, bending sharply. On reaching the fork in it bear left. Go on through the gate and across the field. Bear right, keeping the grass hump just to the left, and then go through the gateway in the wall. Then make for the point ahead where the walls on the wood boundaries on the left and right appear to converge. Go through the gate, and along a track to a quiet road. Turn right and make for the village church at Finsthwaite. In the churchyard is an interesting grave, that of 'Clementina Johannes Sobiesky Douglass, of Waterside' (1771). The presence of a 'Polish princess' here was once something of a mystery but it is now assumed that the lady, who lived quietly near here, was the illegitimate daughter of 'Bonnie Prince Charlie' by his mistress Clementina Walkenshaw, god-daughter of his mother, Clementina Sobiesky.

Take the road past the village school nearby. The road quickly changes to a footpath at an odd stile. Make for the gateway in the field ahead and on to the wicket gate. Follow the track then through the wood and downhill. This brings us onto the road again, but the more hazardous sections have been avoided. Turn right and Lakeside steamer pier is soon reached.

When everyone arrived in Windermere by rail and bus, Orrest Head was a 'must' for all. Now that most visitors arrive by their own transport to Windermere they are off each day to further places and the viewpoint does not get the attention it so deserves. This walk is only a mile and a half but there is a very gradual zig-zag climb that takes up time. Allow one hour for a gentle walk, plus viewing time.

Park on a Windermere car park, and walk up towards the railway station. Instead of turning right to enter the station, cross the main road and look for a small turning which runs upwards to the left of the hotel. The track is tarmaced; a short way up is a footpath sign with two arms, one pointing left and one ahead. Go ahead, up a winding track up the hill. As you ascend the view opens up on the right. There is a view of the lake across the roofs of the village. This tarmac lane zig-zags for most of the way to the summit through a mixed woodland. Beyond a cottage there is an open area to the right and the tarmac gives way to a rough stone track. Presently the track breaks into three. All the ways lead to the summit, but the easiest route is the right hand one following a wall, and slanting off to the corner of another wall. Pause here and enjoy the view of the lake, backed by the fells of the Coniston Old Man range. Just across the lake are the wooded heights of Claife. Towards the right of this is a clear summit crowned by a slim cairn. This is Latterbarrow. Keeping to the right hand path beside a wall we pass through some fine beech trees. Unfortunately for beech trees their smooth bark is an attraction for initial carvers. Ignore the iron gate at right and continue up towards the corner of the wall.

At the wall corner bear right between the wall and a wire fence past some wooden seats. Our objective can now be seen on the grassy crag on the left — the 'pulpit', the summit view indicator. Continue until an iron kissing-gate is reached on the left. Beside is a stone stating that this land was presented for the benefit of the public in memory of one Arthur Heywood. Go through the kissing-gate and straight ahead to the left of the tree towards the pulpit. Take care in ascending the grass as it can be slippery.

The indicator may, or may not, have a diagram illustrating the view depending upon who was first here — the vandal or the reader. In case it was the former the view is as follows: Directly in front the summit of Coniston Old Man (2,631 feet) and the big shoulder to its right is Wetherlam (2,502 feet). Then comes the crinkles of Crinkle

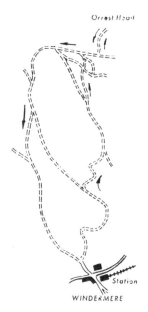

Crags, just a little to the right, and in front of the Pike o'Blisco. If the view is very clear a glimpse of the Scafells is behind, though appearing somewhat dwarfed by their distance away—some fourteen miles. Scafell Pike is the highest point in England (3,206 feet). The summit of nearer Bowfell (2,960 feet) is to the right. Esk Pike is right of this, and if visibility allows, the northern shoulder of the Scafells, Great End (2,984 feet). The familiar Langdale Pikes come next and then, behind, the long ridge of High Raise and Ullscarf. Turning right again the top of the Fairfield Horseshoe can be seen above Wansfell. Right again to the head of Troutbeck is the High Street range. Right again, to look easterly, there are the Yorkshire fells with the flat top of Ingleborough very prominent.

To return, go back to the kissing-gate, but this time instead of going through the beech trees take the path going fairly steeply down beside a wall. This wall marks the boundary of the wood and is followed all the way back. The path winds gradually left, sometimes between two mossy walls, and eventually comes out at the signpost seen on the way up—only this time from the other side.

Gummer's How is an eminence at the foot of Windermere on the eastern shore. It is an excellent viewpoint, and although it is a rough-looking fell it is so placed in relation to a high road that its summit can be reached with little effort by anyone. A healthy person could walk from the road to the top in about fifteen minutes, but would not enjoy the experience as much as the stroller who relishes what he sees. There are one or two rocky steps which must be taken with care by the elderly. Allow plenty of time for members of your party who are unsure of balance or short of wind.

The approach road is about seven miles from Bowness, off the Newby Bridge and Ulverston road. It runs off sharply left after Fell Foot is passed—this is the point in the journey south where the steamer pier at Lakeside is glimpsed across the lake. The road is signed 'Kendal'.

From Newby Bridge, travelling towards Bowness, the road is after one mile; the third turning on the right. There is a stone sign built into wall pointing to 'Kendal'.

The road is very steep. Near the top of the road park in one of the higher lay-bys on the left—second, third or fourth—and walk up to the wooden stile over the wall, leading onto a wide path.

You pass a larch plantation on the right, then after this some old larches are seen scattered about, misshapen by the prevailing wind. Most of them have more than one trunk owing to the leading stem having been damaged by the weather.

The path begins to steepen after a small beck. There are soon good views back along the river Leven to Greenodd and beyond. If it is clear Ingleton, on the Pennines, is seen to the right. The path goes steeper and there are some rock steps. They can all be avoided in their worst places by a detour right or left. The important thing is to take your time and pick out the best route.

As the summit is neared the bracken gives way to heather. There is a triangulation pillar erected by the gentlemen of the Ordnance Survey on the highest point. This is not the best viewing point though there are good views south across Morecambe Bay, and if it is clear enough, one could find Blackpool Tower and rejoice that one is not among its wicked fleshpots.

The best viewpoint is some few yards away from the summit towards the lake. This is spectacular. The pier below looks quite small and the steamers like toys. Almost the whole sweep of the lake can be seen except for the last mile or so which are obscured by

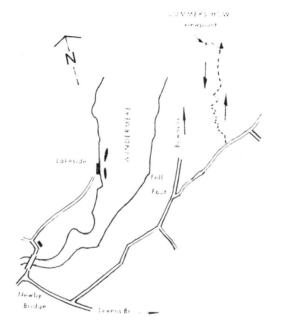

Walk 22

Claife Heights. The round fell far off to the left is Black Coombe on the Cumbrian coast. The small pointed peak to the right, and nearer, has the peculiar name of Caw. Next there is the large Coniston Old Man range with the fierce peaked crag on the left called Dow Crag which has been famous for its rock climbs since the early days of the sport. Right of that are the Langdale Fells, the Helvellyn Fells, Fairfield, and right to High Street range. Esthwaite Water can be seen clearly.

Take care on the way down, choosing the best route to suit you. The area is not open to the public, and the only right of way is the way you came up.

This is a walk for connoisseurs of the countryside. Lancashire's Lake District consists very largely of woodland as it has back to pre-history. Grey and green-lichened crags bulge out of the fields and low moors that break up the woods. Landowners since last century have varied and mellowed the scene by adding artificial tarns and softwood plantations. This walk, which passes by two delightful tarns, is rather typical, and there are fine views across the unspoilt Winster valley. Allow plenty of time for dawdling to drink in the prospects, watch the buzzards wheeling and enjoy the tranquility of the old chapel of St Anthony's o' the Fell. The walk passes through farm land. Dogs disturb stock. If you must take your dog it must be on a lead.

Drive up the road above the Gummer's How footpath. (See previous walk.) On descending the other side a little way, a road will be seen on the right. Drive down it until a place can be found to park on the verge, without obstructing entrances. Walk down the road to the farm yard of Sow How, go through the gate at the end, and soon there is a good track left across the field. Take this until you reach the tarn. This is an artificial lake, but it is a gem none the less, backed attractively by mixed woodland. This tarn, and the next, are private property, so if the weather is hot do not be tempted to jump in.

Walk along the dam and round towards the boathouse. Children will notice that it has a pig weather vane. Go on through the gap in the wall. The track leads up towards a wood and through a gate. Ignore this gate and pick up the path that leaves and bends right, parallel with the wall, to go through a gate ahead into another wood. Tree spotters who are confused with pine and larch will note that the pines on the left through this gate have a red bark and evergreen bluish needles. The larches farther along have rough brown barks and light-green needles which they drop in winter. Bend right round the swamp to the second tarn.

This tarn is another beauty. It is tiny but the background of reeds, willows, silver birch and alder, with the far back-cloth of larch and spruce, make it an attractive miniature. The path again goes along the dam and shortly joins a lane. Turn left into the wood. The tree mixture here is of spruce and douglas fir, with one cyprus tree on the left as the track is joined.

Go through the gate at the end into the field. Follow the wall on the right until a lane is reached turning sharply right to a large barn.

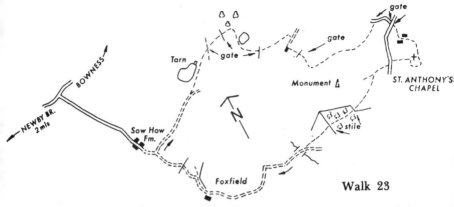

Walk 23

As you walk on past the barn you will notice a pleasant view right, to the end of the Winster valley. (The Winster is the old boundary between Lancashire and Westmorland.) Go through the gate onto the moor, bearing slightly right, then left. As you go forward the view opens up right across the main Winster valley, criss-crossed with dry-stone walls and dotted with old farms. This airy place is the haunt of buzzards, our largest bird of prey next to the golden eagle. They can be recognised by their large flat wings, their end feathers spread like the fingers of a hand. Their flight is in long sweeping circles with hardly a wing movement. Their cry is a high mew, rather like a gull's but sharper and wilder.

The fell on the right of the background is Whitbarrow. Go through gate and follow the track down to another gate. Cross the macadam road and go through the gate opposite. There is a ruin left and a barn right. Go to left of the barn and then go up the bank and in wall slightly left there is a stone 'pinch' stile, otherwise known as a 'fat man's agony'. Go through it, walk towards the wall gap and you will see the roof of what you might assume is another barn. A closer approach through the wall gap will reveal that this is in fact the little church of St Anthony of Cartmel Fell, built in the sixteenth century when the local fell folk built their houses—and their churches—solid and square like their barns. There is a mounting-block and hitching post in the church yard. Go into the church which has some fifteenth-century glass and some glass of unknown antiquity. There is also a three-decker pulpit and some old pews. Children will again note that the stained-glass picture of Saint Anthony bears the picture of a pig. There is literature about the church available inside.

Leave the churchyard by the lychgate and walk past the school. The shine on some of the rock outcrops opposite is not glaciation. It has been put there by generations of children's sliding bottoms, for this was the children's playground. Alas, the children are now taken by bus to a larger school, with more formal and probably much less interesting playgrounds. Follow the road up, until it joins a road at the hill top. Turn left. A gate will shortly be seen into a field on the right. There is a path going towards a monument above Rainsbarrow Old Man. Ignore this path. Go left towards the wood, and follow the wall upwards as the path is indistinct. Just short of the hill summit there is a stile of 'throughs' — that is, long slates which go right through the wall and are put in like steps. Over the stile is a distinct track into the pleasant wood — hardwoods scattered with yew trees, which are common in these parts. Follow the track through and leave the wood via the stile with the iron bar. Very slightly left ahead is a green track which soon joins a hard distinct track. Follow this, right. The bridge a short way along here is a typical fell bridge, built solidly with two culverts. Join the quiet macadam road and bear right through Foxfield Farm buildings, and on along a hard-core track by some very artistic rock outcrops. This track leads to Sow How and the lane where the car is parked.

O.S. 1:50,000 Sheets Nos. 90 and 97

Most motorists travel all the way to Tarn Hows by car. By comparison only a tiny fraction of the Tarn Hows visitors arrive by the pretty route up Glen Mary on foot. Yet this is an extremely fine way to reach what is commonly regarded as the supreme gem of the area. This is the way to go the first time, when the tarn will spring to your view at the top of the waterfalls of Glen Mary, like a climax to a pretty overture. Motorists who already know Tarn Hows, however, can see it all in a new light by this route.

The start is by Glen Mary bridge. From Coniston take the Ambleside road. After the junction left at a mile and a half for Tilberthwaite, the road bends right, there is another left junction and a bridge is crossed. Then it bends left again to cross a little bridge, and there is immediately an open area among the trees on the right. This is where you park. From Ambleside you take the Coniston road. After about four and a half miles there is a little tarn close to the road side on the right. (Yewtree Tarn). A quarter of a mile on, the open place among the trees can be seen on the left.

Walk to the beck and follow it upwards by the path on its right bank. This soon crosses a slate bridge over a little feeder beck, then follows the beck left. Soon you are alongside some pretty waterfalls. Take care if you divert to see them, as there is some very wet ground. Path now goes up rocks. Take care if they are wet. Above these waterfalls, cross the beck by the wooden footbridge, and follow the beck up on the other bank. There are some lovely tall oak trees in this valley. After a short while there is a more impressive waterfall. The path falls a little towards it by oaks that are clinging to the crag sides. Then the path rises and zig-zags to follow the beck. Near the top there is a large crag, with so large an overhang on it that one could shelter under it. Children in the party could no doubt imagine that this is the spot for an Indian ambush. Keep to the left of the beck over rocky steps and you are soon by a little dam. Climb up the track to its top and you are at the tarn.

Turn right and cross the little dam. The best views of the tarn are from the crags which you see beyond the tarn, forward and left, as you stand on the dam. Turn left at the end of the dam and continue on climbing steadily and cunningly not losing height as you go. You should then find a stile high in the fence just below the furthest car park. On the highest little crag is a simple boulder engraved with the names of the donors of the area to the National Trust — the Scott family who gave it in memory of Sir James and Lady Scott in 1930.

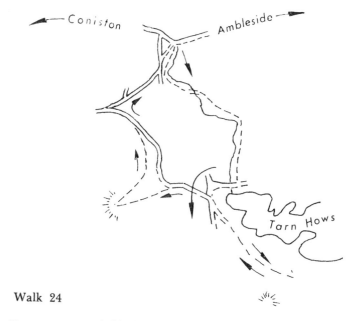

Walk 24

Retrace steps and this time go on to the road at the head. Follow the road, right, past the car parks. After the last car park, and the finish of the wall on the left, there is a path up the hill to the left. Take this path and you will see several little craggy summits ahead. Choose one that has a good view of the length of Coniston Lake. Do not go as far as the cairn on the farthest point, as this is out of the way, and the view is a disappointment. After viewing, turn right about and go back for some distance, then lose height to the left by one of the many little paths. If you can see Yewtree Tarn, by the roadside in the valley bottom, aim towards that. This should bring you back comfortably to the Tarn Hows road again.

Turn left along the road. Go along it until you see the farmhouse of Tarn Hows on the right. As you near it you will see a road leading to it, through a gate on the right. Immediately right of this is a lane turning sharply right with the wall, downhill. Take this lane and it will bring you to the point where you parked the car. Near the bottom of the lane, on the right, are three fine Scots Pines.

O.S. 1:50,000 Sheets Nos. 90 and 97

This is really a rough fell walk. But given good weather — that is very important — and allowing plenty of time, anyone can manage it. Do not walk this alone unless you leave word with someone of the route you are taking. Injured ankles are not unusual on rough ground, and if you do not return to base someone has to know where to find you! Having given these grim warnings it remains to be said that the walk is a splendid little adventure, and highly recommended.

You will need to park at Shepherd's Bridge. This is a little short of two miles north-east of Coniston. From Coniston take the Ambleside road. The first turning left, after about a mile and three quarters, is the Tilberthwaite road. Very shortly afterwards, after the right-hand bend, is the turning for Hodge Close. Turn left down it and after a few yards there are parking places on the grass left and right. From Ambleside take the Coniston road. After about five miles there is a little tarn on the right of the road (Yewtree Tarn.) Just after this the road turns right, and shortly again the Hodge Close turning is seen on the right, Turn right down it. Take care when you park not to pull on to wet ground. If you must, however, drive on frontways so that the driving wheels are near the road edge. (Front wheel drive vehicles vice versa.)

Having parked walk on up the road and cross the little bridge, Shepherd's Bridge. Then immediately afterwards turn right and go through the gate. Follow the track alongside the wall and go through another gate. Follow the wall round, through another gate and bear right, then the track rises slightly left between broken walls. It then follows a wall on the right and goes through another gate. When the wall finishes, and there is a fence leading to another gate, with some pine trees on the knoll to the right, this is where the track is left for a footpath. Do not go through the gate. Turn left and follow the wall upwards. Path bears left away from wall soon by a mountain ash tree. The path goes between a knoll on the left and a swampy area on the right. It continues to the left of the bog, and goes through a little gully among silver birches. It then bends left through junipers, and goes through a gate. The path goes through open woodland among boulders, and begins to climb after a small beck. After the first steep step the path takes a gentler incline and as it approaches a large boulder there is a good view of Yewtree Tarn below on the right.

At the big boulder, bear left up the path which continues to climb.

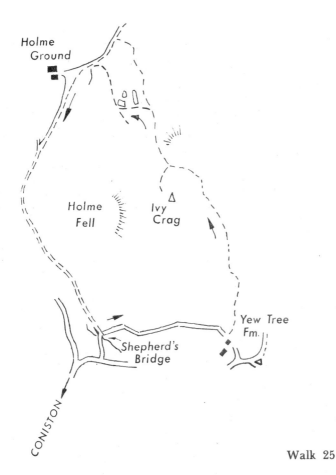

At steep places there is loose rock. Take care not to kick this down on to the people behind. Note 'razor-strop' fungus on the dead birches here. Path eventually bears left, follows a little stream, and then fords it. Path rises following another stream up a small ravine. As you top the ravine a view of Langdale Pikes opens up in front. Continue over a broken wall and a little further on there is a view right to a little tarn. Just as the path begins to descend, a cairn will be seen, left, on the top of a crag. This is Ivy Crag. If you are out of breath rest a little now for Ivy Crag is the next point to visit.

The ascent to the crag, however, is optional. Members of a party who are near exhaustion can rest here and wait for the more energetic to return, as they will come back off the crag to this point.

Turn left and commence the ascent. On nearing the crag do not attempt to scale the bare rock; continue on to the right of it and walk right past it to make the easy ascent from the far side. From the cairn can be seen almost the entire length of Coniston Water. The cairn on the top of Coniston Old Man can be seen right front. Wetherlam is on the right of this and nearer. This leg of the mountain dominates a great deal of the southern Lake District scene. From here it looks gigantic. Right of Wetherlam are Crinkle Crags, Pike o'Blisco, Bowfell, Glaramara in the distance, then Langdale Pikes and Pavey Ark. Then there are the heights of Ullscarf, Steel Fell is nearer, then there is a gap before the hump of Helvellyn. To right is the gap of Grisedale, then the Fairfield range. The grand view is enhanced by the roughness of the near view around. This is an eagle's-eye view of the district. The exploration of the other summits of Holme Fell is *not* recommended. Retrace your steps, and descend by the same route as the ascent, to the path going towards the little tarn.

Continue down towards the tarn, skirt a little crag, then cross through a wet area, through bog myrtle. (Crush some of its leaves, and smell. The herb was once valued by countrywomen to give a fresh pleasant smell to bed sheets.) On nearing the tarn bear left and cross the boggy section approaching its banks. The pretty little tarn is a place to sit for a while.

Turn left from the point at which you reach the tarn, and continue on this line through a little gap, which brings you to a broken dam with another little tarn on the right. Cross the dam, and turn left under the trees; this picks up a faint path which rises slightly and then joins another, better, path at a T junction. Turn right. This path breasts a small rise, then descends and curves left. Here there is a grove of rowans, or mountain ash trees. Rowans are usually solitary and it is unusual to find them in groves. Their wood was once much valued to keep away witches. One beam of mountain ash had to be put among the oak beams of the houses of old, between the door and the hearth, to prevent free passage of witches. A cross of rowan was also often erected by the door to keep away evil.

The path becomes quite distinct. At wall turn left and go through the gate. Follow a track alongside the wall. It leaves the wall and continues to descend. Ignore sharp turn right to the cottages, but go onwards with wall. Skirt the wet ground and go through gate. Beyond the gate take to the higher ground left to avoid more wetness. The track eventually joins the road; continue left. Follow this road, which follows the ghyll right back to Shepherd's Bridge, and your car.

O.S. 1:50,000 Sheet No. 90

Tilberthwaite is reached from Coniston by the first turning left, after one mile, on the Ambleside road. From Ambleside it is the second turning right after passing the roadside tarn on the Coniston road, after 4½ miles.

Park in the levelled area at Tilberthwaite ghyll foot, just before the bridge. The walk starts over the bridge, past the cottages and round to the farm (High Tilberthwaite Farm). Pass through the farmyard and go through the gate on the left, which leads onto a fell track. When the rising ground begins to flatten look back at the view of the ravine of Tilberthwaite Ghyll. Go on up through the gorse. There should be at least some of it in bloom in any month, summer or winter. Hence the saying 'When gorse is in bloom, kissing is in season'.

Ahead the Fairfield mountain range comes into view. There are quarries all around. One big one can be seen across the valley to the right. Go round curve left through gate, and on through another gate. The quarries up the left were used in the last century by a notorious rogue called 'Lantly Slee', who distilled illicit whisky in secret places. One of his little caves is up above, but it cannot be found unless you know where to look. On the track summit the hump of Lingmoor, across Little Langdale, can be seen and one has the impression of being really high. As the corner is turned one can see Langdale Pikes — Harrison Stickle looms over the left shoulder of Lingmoor. Keep right on. On brow before descent, Little Langdale Tarn can be seen below. Down through the gate, and further left — and Fell Foot Farm can be seen and above it left a stretch of Wrynose Pass. The road from this view looks impassable, and an impossible feat of engineering. But it has been there for something like nineteen hundred years — the Romans built the original.

As the wall on the right curves off it is possible for people in a hurry to cut the corner with it for the way is below, right. But who is in a hurry? The track down to the hairpin is pleasant, with the view ahead.

Turn right to nearby farm buildings by the large yew tree. Ford stream and go through gate past it. To the right the quarry waste is piled high but the slate colours are mellowed by moss and lichen. Descend to the group of farm buildings and the track levels. Watch for the first ash tree by the wall on the right, and opposite it is a worn and tricky stile. Climb it and walk towards stone footbridge.

This is one of the most photographed sketched bridges in the

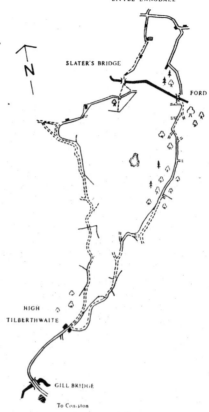

LITTLE LANGDALE

SLATER'S BRIDGE

FORD

N

HIGH
TILBERTHWAITE

GILL BRIDGE

To Coniston

Walk 26

Lake District, and a look at it will explain why. It is known as
'Slaters Bridge', and was built by the quarrymen long ago. It
seems to have grown out of the ground. Here is a place to linger.

Cross the bridge and follow the track up alongside the wall. From
the top of its rise you have the best view of Little Langdale valley,
with the tarn in foreground, the pass above, and to the left the great
northern shoulders of the Coniston Old Man range with Wetherlam
directly above. The great narrow valley leading to its head is
Greenburn, a place of abandoned mines, for copper has been mined
in these fells since the days of the Romans. Go on through the stile,
and through gates alongside the farm to the lane. Turn left. Enjoy
the view, left, as you go.

This lane joins the Little Langdale-Wrynose road. Turn right.
There is only a little way to go on this road, which is as well as a good

look out is needed for the traffic. After a couple of minutes you are in the village of Little Langdale, a post office, an inn and little else. After the cottages on right, turn right down lane. At the foot of the lane there is a group of terraced cottages known locally as 'Jam Row' for the miners formerly who lived there were so poor that it was said their entire diet consisted of bread and home-made jam. Just before the ford and footbridge the footpath is built up at a higher level to allow passage in floods. Onto footbridge. The ford below is really a horse-and-cart ford. Occasionally cars try it in spite of warning notices and you may find one stuck in the middle.

At the other side go through gate ahead and bear right. The road is clear and follows the wall on the right. Through another gate. Once again this is a world of quarries. Yet the spoil heaps are not all ugly. Note how the birch trees quickly take over. They are the pioneer trees seeding where there seems to be no soil at all, and their fallen leaves give nourishment for green ground-cover.

Follow the more distinct path all the way (branch right at fork) and climb upwards, then on past some old trees back to the farmyard of High Tilberthwaite, Tilberthwaite Ghyll lying right ahead.

This is a woodland walk through the northern end of Grizedale Forest. Woodland walks are often regarded as poor-weather walks, but it would be a pity if this walk were marred by poor visibility as it has fine views at various points. In winter snows it is fine. From June through August walkers need to carry insect repellent. The walk has a few wet sections which can be avoided with careful navigation. It finishes with a climb on a minor road which need not be a flog if plenty of time is allowed to stroll it. Smokers should take great care not to start fires!

Leave Coniston by the Hawkshead road, and when you are almost at the crown of the hill a road junction to the right can be seen with a horse-trough and ornamental fountain near it. Just after this look for the large quarry on the left. This is no longer worked and it gives plenty of room to park your car. Leave the car, go onto the road and turn left to climb it further. Presently a road junction left is seen, signposted 'Ambleside & Tarn Hows'. Your way is opposite to it, through a gateway into the forest. Go up the forest road. For a good portion of the journey from now on the way is marked by yellow marks. When the forest road divides, continue right on into the spruce forest. Spruces give way to larch, and at the next junction bear right. The view opens up presently to the right, over Coniston Old Man range.

When the forest road again divides, this time bear left, and continue climbing. At a T junction turn right. Within a few yards there is another junction. The yellow marked route here leaves you to join a red-marked route, left. The red-marked route also goes right. Your way is straight ahead. This is a path rather than a track and follows power lines. Cross the forest road when reached and go right on. Choose your own way through this gash in the forest and the fire tower is reached. This is a land mark for miles—High Man—and this path is a very old right of way. The tower is only manned at fire danger periods. Continue right on. It will be noticed that our way is marked by standing slates which are the remains of an old fence. You pass on the right of a pond. After a wet section with a moss on the left, the way ahead closes in somewhat under some large old larch trees. These are mis-shapen into a forester's nightmare, but at the time of writing have not been felled. Long may they remain as a welcome eccentricity among the military ranks all around them! Shortly after these larches the path falls to reach a forest road which crosses it. You now leave the ridge path and turn left on this road. At the junction bear right; this is followed quickly by another junction, bear right again. Soon this road rises

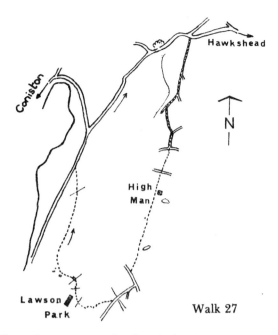

to a brow where there are two fire-breaks in the forest to the left, and one fire break to the right. About 150 yards beyond this look for a path going down to the right leaving this road. If the signpost is there it probably reads 'Brantwood'. Go down this path.

The path wanders, through wet sections, to a gate with good views across Coniston. This is Lawson Park. Go through the gate, turn right, and go through another gate. This is an old track. Descend to a gateway in an old wall. Go over the plank bridge and go upwards, following a wall, which is on the left. There is a barn soon on the left and opposite this point the track rises to the right. The track goes on through broadleaved woodlands. They are mainly birch and oak, but as you descend the varieties are greater. Go through the gate. There are two large beeches beyond it. Go through another gate and over a bridge. Below this gate, and to right, are two middle-aged trees, a holly tree and an ash tree which have grown so closely together that they have become welded into each other. After this there is another gate leading onto a road. Join the road and turn right.

When the road forks take the lesser one, to the right. Some handsome old trees line this road, and the prospects left are lost to the motorists who drive along this road. The road steepens and may seem somewhat stiff. Comfort yourself in the knowledge that when you see the forest entrance road on the right, you are near the end of the journey. You join the road by the horse-trough. Turn right and you are soon at the quarry.

Most of this walk is on uneven ground, and there are wettish sections. There is also some climbing, so although the distance is only three and a half miles it needs rather more time than might be expected. Nevertheless it can be enjoyed by anyone. No Coniston lovers should miss this lake-shore walk, and the views offered by the higher-level return.

Torver is a hamlet south of Coniston village. The inhabitants of Torver will tell you that it is every bit as important as its northern upstart. Leave Coniston by the Ulverston road, the main one south, A593. Torver is reached in about 2½ miles. There is a little church, the Church House Inn, then the road turns right and forks; take the left fork as for Ulverston. After less than ¾ mile there is a garage on the right and the road begins to descend. Watch for an iron fence on the top of a wall on the left, then shortly after this for a grass lay-by on the left. Pull in here. There should be a signpost 'Public footpath Coniston' here. Forward of the lay-by there is a track ascending, bearing left. Walk this way, and go through a gate.

You are now on Torver Back Common which is a public access area managed by the National Park Planning Board, and patrolled by its wardens who are there to help the public to enjoy the area in safety, and to make sure that they do not destroy what they have come to enjoy! When the track forks take the right hand path down to the wall, and you are descending to the lake shore. Avoid the wet section by bearing right slightly. You are soon on a path which follows the lake shore at a slightly higher level. Now if the lake is very low after dry weather it is possible to walk this route by the shingly beach, but keep one eye on the route instructions, which follow the path, or you will probably end up in Coniston, and have a longish trek back. There is no safe bathing, by the way, for non-swimmers, as the lake bed shelves very steeply after a shallow start, and off-shore for a good part of this walk it is over 140 feet deep.

The path leaves the shore slightly to avoid crags, and goes round oak coppice. There are some large juniper bushes along here, mixed in with gorse, and some yew trees. This makes identification by shrub-spotters less easy as they look similar. Gorse are extremely prickly, and you can find their distinctive yellow pea-type flower in any month of the year. (There is an old country saying that when there is no gorse in flower, kissing is out of season.) By comparison juniper is only semi-prickly, grows on larger, stouter stems, flowers in May to June, but with flowers rather small and insignificant, and bears berries here nearly all the year in stages of ripeness from green

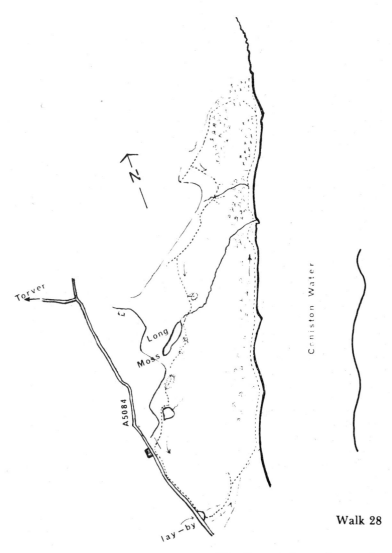

N

Torver

A5084

Long

Moss

Coniston Water

lay-by

Walk 28

to black. A bite at the green one will tell you where gin gets its flavour from. Yew is non-prickly, its early spring flowers are almost invisible, its soft red berries are gobbled by birds. It is a very slow growing tree which made the bows for the bowmen of England. The thickly-growing branches are flat. Some way along the path there is a juniper growing alongside a yew, its branches tangled with it.

Watch for the little crag viewpoint to the lake side of the path which gives a good view south to the softer stretches of the lake. As the wood to the left thickens, the path crosses a boggy section by stepping stones, and when another boggy area is reached the path avoids it by going left and taking a slightly higher contour, before turning down again between junipers and gorse. At a point where the path is crossed by a beck, on shingles to the shore, there should be signs of clinker as this is the site of an old 'bloomery'. There are many old iron mines in the Furness area of the Lake District, and so great was the demand for timber to produce charcoal for smelting that in early times the ore was carried by boat to wooded shores such as this, and crudely smelted. Lumps of the iron slag can be found. So great was the destruction of the woods, that in 1565 all the bloomeries in Furness were suppressed. But the destruction began again in the following century, and continued for two centuries.

The path rises after this beck, and passes left of a crag, and there is now a substantial woodland to the left, nearly all native broad-leaves as little or no planting would have taken place in this area. There is oak, birch, hawthorn and holly, ash and yew. Most of this hardwood is coppice — shoots growing from the roots of a previously felled tree. Ignore forks and follow the path which runs parallel to the shore. The path passes through the remnants of a wall, with the remains of an iron fence into the water. There is then a plantation of larch on the left. (Notice on the dead birch trunks the typical protruding fungi, once used by country folks as razor strops as they are so tough.) By the side of this path as you go along you may find more iron slag from bloomeries. The dry-stone walls of an old hearth can be found in the bank at one point. Spruce, pine, and beech have also been planted along this shore. Another broken wall is reached at the end of the wood, and the way now leads away from the lake shore. Bear left and go across the field, dotted by birch trees, to the gap in a broken wall, where a track will be picked up which follows the fence of a plantation and then turns through an old gateway. Go directly on. At fork keep left and go on with the beck on your right. One or two wet sections can be avoided with care. Take care over slippery wet rock.

Some time after the bog on the right is passed, the path comes close to a stone wall coming in from the right, and a wall can be seen, front. At this point a substantial path turns off very sharply left and rises to the crest of a hill. Take this one. (There is a gate in the wall ahead. If you reach it you have gone too far.) Up this track there is a good view across the lake. The large white house on the opposite shore is Brantwood, which was the home of John Ruskin, political economist, art critic, writer and philosopher, from 1855 to 1900, when he died. Over your left shoulder is the Coniston Old Man range.

The track meanders a little, generally towards the lake. On reaching a little beck the path splits three ways. Take the path on the right which follows the beck up. The wetness can be avoided with care. The path goes through an arch of large junipers, and goes upwards. It then curves left through more junipers, after being joined by a faint path from the right. The head of the lake can be seen from the brow of this hill. The path is to the right of a swamp and curves right through a juniper jungle. (Interesting to see how the shape of junipers varies so tremendously between pancakes and spires.) The path rises parallel with, but some distance from, a wall on the right, then moves nearer to it. When the junipers thin out and there is a rather more dreary prospect of a sea of bracken dotted with a few junipers in front, it is at this point that we leave the path to take a less distinct one up the path to the left. This new path runs parallel with the lake without losing height, and goes towards a little crag outcrop. Make for this and climb it as it is a good viewpoint. Almost the entire length of the lake can be seen.

Having enjoyed this view (assuming there is good visibility) look to the right along the fell and you should see part of a little tarn. A route of sorts can be seen to it from this crag. Keep to the path on the right of the crag and make for this tarn. The path curves left to avoid a swamp, then turns right after crossing a small beck, and rejoins the original line of travel by curving left round an outcrop. The tarn is hidden from view, but there is a hill behind it, with a single mountain-ash tree near its summit; make towards this, and the tarn is soon reached. The tarn is known as Long Moss. Make for our mountain ash hill as there is a quiet pleasant view from it.

The way on is pathless across rough ground, but you should aim in the direction of a stone wall which can be seen to your front if you stand with the tarn on the right. Before reaching the wall go up the small rise on the left. Looking right we can see civilisation again in the shape of an ugly garage. Before making for it go towards the little tarn in front. This is Kelly Hall Tarn. Sitting by this tarn, with the little beck tinkling in at the side, you would hardly know that the road was so near. Rejoining the path at a higher level, it goes to a wall. Follow the wall, keeping it on your right. Go through the gate in the fence and continue to the road side near the garage. Walk left down the side of the road. Avoid being run down by taking to the grass on the left and you are soon back at your car.

The Beacon Tarn walk is a delightful mild fell walk. It is good at any time of year, but needs clear conditions for the proper enjoyment of the views. For the absolute peak of enjoyment it should be walked on a fine clear day with the heather in full bloom. It is then something to remember for many a long day. From Beacon, also visited, the view is excellent.

The worst part of the walk, as always, is planned for the beginning. This is the short section along a rather unsafe public road. This needs care. After this all is well. The walk starts at the car park at Old Brown How public access area (National Park) or just south of this on one of the Blawith Common access area car parks. These points are about five miles south of Coniston on the Ulverston road. After the branch road to Broughton is passed the road winds, then descends a hill to follow close by the lake shore. A walled property eventually intervenes; this is Old Brown How. Watch for the entrance to the car park on the left. Blawith Common is an open area beyond this.

After parking the car, walk on towards Ulverston. After the open common, a property known as Lake Bank is passed. There are one or two blind bends, and it is a good policy to place yourself at the side of the road in a position which can be seen by approaching traffic — eg on the outside of the bend. Take advantage of any verge. Soon there are some buildings on the right, after the road passes through rock cuttings. This is Water Yeat. There is a section of the older road forking off to the right. Take this and walk between the cottages, then turn right at the junction at the end, up a minor macadamed road which runs alongside an old mill race. The road winds, with green farm fields on the left and the bracken-covered common on the right. At the farm the macadam ends and a track continues on past the farm turning. This is the way. There is a wall on the left. The track rises away from the wall at one point, then goes back towards it. It then goes between walls with a broad-leafed wood on the left. A track joins from the left. continue right on. The track soon emerges onto common land, with a wall on the right. When this is passed, you are on the open fell and the track is pleasant and green.

Jump, or ford, a beck and continue on a wettish section. After this the way narrows to a footpath, but is still easily seen on the ground. The path goes over a rise, crosses another wet section, then continues on bearing right. It undulates over rocky mounds clothed in heather and bracken with a little beck on the right. When the

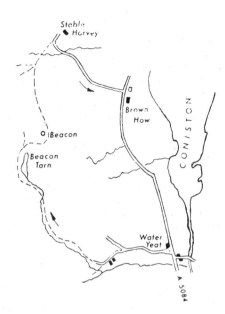

Walk 29

path forks near a little waterfall take the more distinct path, on a higher level, to the left. Skirt the wet section on the right. Follow the path to the left of the beck. When the end of Beacon Tarn comes into view see if you can cross the beck. This will avoid a wet section of the path farther up. If the beck is in spate and cannot be crossed, continue on.

When the tarn is reached, continue along the left-hand bank of it. All this area is open to the public. You can drift about here to your heart's content. But the path goes on along the bank. The tarn is large and is completely natural. At the top of the tarn, cross the beck and continue along the bank. After crossing the top of the tarn go right up the bank of a faint path, for you are now bound for the Beacon, one of the finest viewpoints in the district. The path is not very clear at first, but continue on and up through the heather. Very shortly after climbing, you should see that the natural way to the summit, which is forward and left ahead, is a grassy hollow leading upwards left between heather and bracken clothed rocks. A path can be picked up past a dead hawthorn tree. Looking back the large tarn is seen at its best. The miniature crags behind give the illusion that it is bigger than it is. As this path rises higher, you have a view left to craggy summits, the higher pointed peak being Caw. Right over to the left is the large hump of Black Combe. This is a landmark for sailors.

Take the climb slowly and with patience. Higher up you can see back across Morecambe Bay. The path eventually leads onto a

93

little level area. There is a splendid view of the Coniston Old Man range, and on it is the large scar of the Broughton Moor Quarry which is still in full production. Cross to the rock face to the right, across the wet section. But turn right, and walk below this rock face, then before the little path starts to descend, turn at a sharp angle left up a heathery gully to bring yourself above the crag. As you continue to climb, take a last look at Beacon Tarn as it is not visible from the Beacon. Go forward now on a more distinct path which opens onto a pleasant plateau, and goes up towards the summit through a grassy and heathery dell. The full length of Coniston can be seen on the right. This is one of the best views of the lake. The little island off the wooded promontory is Peel Island. This is the island Arthur Ransome called 'Wild Cat Island' in the well-known book *Swallows and Amazons*. The tarn forward and below is Torver Tarn. The head of the lake looks quite impressive. The fierce-looking crags of Yewdale Fells add to the wildness. The Fairfield range of mountain can be seen beyond in the distance. The High Street range is to the right of this. Right, and back, on a clear day there are views well out over Morecambe Bay and beyond.

From the summit cairn rejoin the path you have left. In other words walk towards Coniston Lake. Then on reaching the path, turn left and carry on down, keeping the lake in view. A steep section is avoided by a little zig-zag right. On reaching a level area the path bears left to the left of a crag outcrop, and the view of the bottom of the lake length is lost. When the path forks, ignore left fork and continue on, on a more distinct path, losing height gradually. This falls left across a wet heathery gully and a little beck. A path is then picked up and you take it, right. It leaves the little beck then zig-zags and becomes more distinct. Nearing the valley floor the path picks up a track. Follow it right towards the macadam minor road. On reaching the road turn right. Follow the road through the common. The common here is dotted with oak, birch and ash, with willows in the wet hollows. If the land was not grazed it would soon become seeded and would be woodland. Most of the trees have escaped being grazed in their seedling stage because they are not very readily accessible to sheep. Some of the oaks are growing out of crags, for instance. There is a nice lone rowan at one point, on the left, which is badly disfigured by initials. Cuts such as these can let in fungi attacks which eventually kill the tree; this tree is sick and slowly dying. As the road falls into hollows, spicy bog myrtle covers the wet ground.

The minor road joins the Coniston to Ulverston road at a T junction near Old Brown How. The car parks are off to the right.

This ought to be walk number one. It brings you a high rim of the Lake District National Park on its eastern boundary. The view is a surprise one. A great deal of what the Lake District has to offer is spread before you. It is like a mammoth shop window. If conditions are right there are views stretching on for twenty miles and more in all directions. It has two other merits: one can lengthen or shorten the walk at will; and the route is dry throughout. In poor visibility or in very strong wind, however, it should not be attempted.

From the centre of Kendal leave by the road opposite the Town Hall (All Hallows Lane) at the traffic lights. Follow this road right up and on towards Underbarrow, crossing the Kendal by-pass. At the top of the hill start the descent, then immediately watch for the entrance to a public car park on the right; Scout Scar car park. Park here, walk back to the road, turn right, and an iron kissing-gate will be seen on the left. Take the right-hand fork beyond the gate, to the top of the hill. Soon we are on the top of a great limestone edge. This is an exposed part of the 250 million years old limestone which encircles the Lake District. Once it extended into the central areas, but great earth movements and the giant forces of erosion broke and scoured it away.

The edge is sharp. It falls away at a precipice, then slopes steeply into the woods. The valley below is the Lyth, famous in the spring for the sight and scent of damson blossom, and a mecca in the late summer for jam and wine makers. The ugly looking structure ahead is the Scout Scar 'mushroom'. This crowns the viewpoint. At one time the ceiling of this oddity had diagrams of the fell outlines, and with their use it was possible to name all the peaks in view. Now it has only the marks of mindless scribblers and the edifice has no function at all. It is useless as a shelter.

The view is fantastic on a clear day. The nearest fells, looking out over the edge, are those of the Coniston Old Man range, a large mass riddled with mine shafts and slashed by quarries. To their right, and farther away, are the Langdale fells, and behind them part of the roof of England—the Scafell range. Right again, the Grasmere fells, then the Fairfield and Helvellyn range, and directly right, the High Street ranges. Behind us are the eastern fells of Cumbria, backed by the fells of Yorkshire. To our left is a view south over Morecambe Bay.

Walking again to the edge and onwards, directly below can be seen how the dark evergreen yew trees have grown well on the

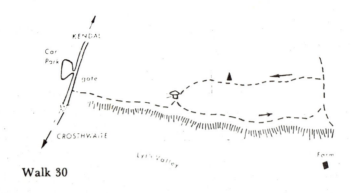

Walk 30

crumbling slopes. They are extremely slow growing, and their hard wood made the bows that once won many battles. The taller trees of evergreen are pines.

Go forward. It is pleasanter taking the green track near the edge of the scar. The soil on the top is very thin and hawthorn and heather have only succeeded in getting a foothold. Stunted ash trees have also found pockets of soil in the cracks and hollows of the limestone. The attraction of this walk is the view westward, but looking back the curves and sharp edges of the scar look impressive. You can walk along here as far as you want, or turn back if you wish; but it is suggested that you walk as far as the point where a track branches off left. This is just above the point overlooking the large farm in the fields at the end of the wood. The point is marked with a cairn. Turn left along this branch track, and walk to the summit of the ridge. Turn left again and follow the ridge which is marked by cairns. Choose to walk on the grass when you can as the rock is very uneven. After a while a 'triangulation pillar', a small concrete platform to which the Ordnance Survey men fix their instruments, is reached. (These points are marked on Ordnance Survey maps by a small triangle.) This is another excellent viewpoint.

From this point go through the gap in the wall, and walk back to the car park by way of the mushroom and the kissing-gate.